DAVE BARRY SLEPT HERE

A Sort of History of the United States

DAVE BARRY
SLEPT HERE

Dave Barry

Random House   New York

For Robert,
who really *was* born
on October 8

Library of Congress Cataloging-in-Publication Data

Barry, Dave
Dave Barry slept here.

1. United States–History–Humor. I. Title
E178.4.B27   1989   973'.0207   88-43205
ISBN 0-394-56541-X

Manufactured in the United States of America

24689753

FIRST EDITION

Book design by Carole Lowenstein

CONTENTS

INTRODUCTION

"WE THE PEOPLE." These are the words that begin the Declaration of Independence. Or maybe we are thinking of the Gettysburg Address. No matter. The point is, these words are written on an extremely historic yellowed document that we, as a nation, keep in a special vault in Washington, D.C., where, each working day, it is cherished by employees of the Document Cherishing Division of the Federal Bureau of Historic Yellowed Objects.

And with good reason. For these three words remind us that we live in a nation that was built by *human beings*. It is easy to forget this, especially when we are riding in the coach section of a commercial aircraft, sitting on seats apparently built by and for alien beings who are fourteen inches tall and capable of ingesting airline "omelets" manufactured during the Korean War (1949–1953). At times like this, it is important that we look back at the people and the events that got us to where we are today, for, in the words of a very wise dead person, "A nation that does not know its history is doomed to do poorly on the Scholastic Aptitude Test."

And that was the main reason why we wrote this book, aside from wanting to become so wealthy that we shall routinely leave motor yachts as tips. Tragically, many Americans know very little about the history of their own country. We constantly see surveys that reveal this ignorance, especially among our high school students, 78 percent of whom, in a recent nationwide multiple-choice test, identified Abraham Lincoln as "a kind of lobster." That's right: more than *three quarters* of our nation's youth could not correctly identify the man who invented the telephone.

What is the cause of this alarming situation? Partly, of course, it is that our young people are stupid. Young people have *always* been stupid, dating back to when *you* were a young person (1971–1973) and you drank an entire quart of Midnight Surprise Fruit Wine and Dessert Topping and threw up in your best friend's father's elaborate saltwater aquarium containing $6,500 worth of rare and, as it turned out, extremely delicate fish. (You thought we didn't know about that? We know *everything*. We are a history book.)

But another major part of the problem is the system used to teach history in our schools, a system known technically, among professional educators, as the Boring Method. You were probably taught via this method, which features textbooks that drone on eternally as follows:

EARLY EXPLORATIONS

The region was first explored by the Spanish explorer Juan Ponce de Rigeur (1534–1579), who in 1541 was commissioned by King Charles "Chuck" IV of England (1512–1583) under the terms of the Treaty of Weems (1544) as authorized by Pope Bilious XIV (1511–1598) to end the Nine Years, Three Months, and the Better Part of a Week War (May 4, 1534–August 8, 1543, at about 1:30 P.M.), under which France (1243–present) would cede an area "north of the 17th parallel, west of the 163rd longitude, and convenient to shopping" to England in exchange for those lands originally conquered by Denmark during the Reign of Large Unattractive Feathered Hats (1387–1396) and subsequently granted to Italy under the Treaty of . . .

And so on. Little wonder that our young people choose to ignore their nation's history and instead focus their intellectual energies on procuring designer clothing. Not that you, the reader, should feel superior. You are probably not such a history whiz yourself. In fact, we are willing to bet that you cannot even name the man who served as Gerald Ford's running mate in 1976.[1] Which is why it is a darned good thing for all concerned that this book has been published. Because this book does not waste the reader's valuable brain cells with such trivial details as when various events actually occurred. Oh, sure, it contains many exact dates—it is, after all, a history book—but you will notice that we have tried to make these dates as easy as possible to remember by making them all start with "October 8," as in "October 8, 1729," or "October 8, 1953." We chose this particular date after carefully weighing a number of important historical criteria, such as (a) it is our son's birthday.

In our view, the one-date system of history has the same advantages, in terms of simplifying things, as the metric system of measurement, which has taken this country by storm, and we look forward to the day when history textbooks carry this system even further and contain only one *year,* so that a child will be able to get all the way through the secondary educational system without ever having to grasp any concept other than "October 8, 1947."[2] And that is only one of the many revolutionary advances contained here. Another one is: *We have left out the dull parts.*

[1] It doesn't matter.
[2] We were born in 1947.

Take, for example, the Role of the Plow in the Settlement of Nebraska. "The hell with the Role of the Plow in the Settlement of Nebraska"—that is our motto. This philosophy left us with plenty of extra room, which enabled us to provide you, the reader, with large, restful expanses of white space, as well as numerous riveting "behind-the-scenes" historical anecdotes that you will not find in a normal history book because we made them up.

In conclusion, we hope that, in reading this work, you gain a deeper and broader and taller understanding of how We, the People, through the sweat of our armpits, created this great nation, a nation of which it can truly be stated, in the words of the famous folk singer Woody Guthrie[3]:

> *This land is your land,*
> *This land is my land,*
> *Looks like one of us*
> *Has a forged deed to this land.*

[3]October 8, 1912–October 8, 1967.

DAVE BARRY SLEPT HERE

CHAPTER ONE

Deflowering
a Virgin
Continent

HUNDREDS of thousands of years ago,
America was very different. There was no
civilization: no roads, no cities, no shopping malls,
no Honda dealerships. There were, of course, obnoxious shouting radio *commercials* for car dealerships; these have been broadcast toward Earth for
billions of years by the evil Planet of Men Wearing Polyester Sport Coats, and there is nothing
anybody can do to stop them. But back then, you
see, there was no way to *receive* them, so things
were pretty peaceful.

The only inhabitants of America in those days
were animals such as the deer and the antelope,
who were engaged primarily in playing; and the

buffalo, or "bison,"[1] who mainly roamed. The bison must have been an awe-inspiring sight: millions of huge, majestic animals, forming humongous herds, their hooves thundering like, we don't know, thunder or something, roaming from the Mississippi River all the way across the Great Plains to the Rocky Mountains, which they would smash into headfirst at speeds ranging upward of thirty-five miles per hour, then fall down. They were majestic, those bison, but stupid.

But all of this changed twenty thousand years ago with the construction of the Land Bridge to Asia, which was completed on October 8. Suddenly, the ancestors of the Indians and the Eskimos, clans who called themselves "The Ancestors of the Indians and the Eskimos," had a way to get to North America. Still, it was not an easy trek: They had to traverse hundreds of miles of frigid snow-swept wasteland, which was cold, and each was permitted to carry only two small pieces of luggage. Eventually they arrived in an area very near what we now know as Kansas, and they saw that it was a place of gently rolling hills and clear flowing streams and abundant fertile earth, and they looked upon this place, and they said, "Nah."[2] Because quite frankly they were looking for a little more action, which is how come they

[1]Meaning "buffalo."
[2]"No."

ended up on the East Coast. There they formed tribes and spent the next several thousand years thinking up comical and hard-to-spell names for major rivers. Also they made a great many Native American handicrafts such as pots, although at the time there was not much of a retail market for these, so the Native Americans wound up having to use them as household implements.

During this same period another group of early Americans, the Mayans, were constructing a culture down in Mexico featuring a calendar so advanced that it can still, to this very day, tell you where various celestial bodies such as Venus and the Moon will be at any given moment. *They will be out in space,* states the miraculous Mayan calendar.

Meanwhile, way the hell far away in someplace like Finland, Vikings were forming. These were extremely rugged individuals whose idea of a fun time was to sail over and set fire to England, which in those days was fairly easy to ignite because it had a very high level of thatch, this being the kind of roof favored by the local tribespeople—the Klaxons, the Gurnseys, the Spasms, the Wasps, the Celtics, and the Detroit Pistons. No sooner would they finish thatching one when the Vikings, led by their leader, Eric the Red (so called because that was his name), would come charging up, Zippos blazing, and that would be the end of *that* roof. This went on for thousands of years, during which time the English tribespeople became very oppressed, not to mention damp.

Then there arose among them a young man who many said would someday become the king of all of England because his name was King Arthur. According to legend, one day he was walking along with some onlookers, when he came to a sword that was stuck in a stone. He grasped the sword by the handle and gave a mighty heave, and to the amazement of the onlookers, he suddenly saw his shadow, and correctly predicted that there would be six more weeks of winter. This so impressed the various tribes that Arthur was able to unite them and drive off the Vikings via the bold and resourceful maneuver of serving them relentlessly bland food, a tradition that remains in England to this day despite numerous armed attempts by the French to invade with sauces.

Thus it was that the Vikings set off across the Atlantic in approximately the year 867—on October 8—to (a) try to locate North America and (b) see if it was flammable. Did these hardy adventurers reach the New World centuries before Columbus? More and more, historians argue that they did, because this would result in a new national holiday, which a lot of historians would get off. But before we can truly know the answer to this question, we must do a great deal more research. And quite frankly, we would rather not.

DISCUSSION QUESTIONS

1. Would *you* buy a car from a dealership that ran one of those obnoxious shouting radio commercials? Neither would we.
2. Have you noticed that you hardly ever see Zippo lighters anymore? Explain.
3. Are you aware that there is a traditional British dish called "cock-a-leeky soup"? Really.

CHAPTER TWO

Spain
Gets Hot

FOR MANY HUNDREDS of years, European traders had dreamed of discovering a new route to the East, but every time they thought they had found it, they would start whimpering, and their wives would wake them up. So they continued to use the old route, which required them to cross the Alps on foot, then take a sailing ship across the Mediterranean to Egypt, then take a camel across the desert, then take *another* sailing ship *back* across the Mediterranean, then change to the IRT Number 6 Local as far as 104th Street, and then ask directions. Thus it would often take them years to get to the East, and when they finally did, they were almost always disappointed. "This is *it*?" they would say. "This is the *East*?"

And so by the fifteenth century, on October 8, the Europeans were looking for a new place to try to get to, and they came up with a new concept: the West. The problem here was that the immediate west was covered with the Atlantic Ocean, which represented a major obstacle because back in those days many people believed that the world was flat. Today, of course, we know that this is true only in heavily Protestant states such as Iowa, but back then people believed that if you went too far, you might sail right off the edge. In fact, you would probably *want* to sail off the edge, since the average sailing ship had about the same size and seaworthiness as a Yugo hatchback.

THE FORTUNATE INVENTION OF CERTAIN NAVIGATIONAL AIDS

Then, fortunately, along came the invention of certain navigational aids. Chief among these was a very realistic doll that, when you inflated it, could . . . WAIT! Wrong kind of aid! Our mistake! Chief among the navigational aids was the compass, a device that, no matter where it is, always indicated which way was north. This was a tremendous boon to early navigators, although its value was diminished somewhat by the fact that the early voyages always ended with the ship banging into the polar ice cap and everybody aboard freezing to death. But eventually the compass was improved by the addition of such fea-

tures as: south, west, and even east again, and
soon hardy[1] mariners were able to venture far out
into the Atlantic before getting lost. Still, it was
difficult to recruit new sailors, even with the use
of extensive advertising campaigns built around
catchy themes such as:

BE ALL THAT YOU CAN BE!
Become a Hardy Mariner
"Get Lost and Die."

Eventually the breakthrough came that made
modern navigation possible: the discovery of lon-
gitudes and latitudes. These are thin black lines
that go all around Earth in a number of locations,
so that all you have to do is follow them, and you
have a surefire way of getting wherever it is they
go. Of course they are difficult for the untrained
eye to see; the early sailors had to squint at the
water for hours, which is why so many of them
ended up having to wear eye patches, especially in
movies. But the hardy sacrifice those early mariners made for us will never be forgotten, not as
long as we are reading this particular paragraph.

Meanwhile, in nearby Italy, Christopher Columbus was forming. As a youth, he spent many
hours gazing out to sea and thinking to himself:
"Someday I will be the cause of a holiday ob-
served by millions of government workers." The

---

[1]In the sense of, "not tremendously bright."

fact that he thought in English was only one of the amazing things about the young Columbus. Another was his conviction that if he sailed all the way across the Atlantic, he would reach India. We now know, thanks to satellite photographs, that this makes him seem as stupid as a buffalo, although it sounded pretty good when Columbus explained it to the rulers of Spain, Ferdinand and his lovely wife, Imelda, who agreed to finance the voyage by selling six thousand pairs of her shoes.

And so Columbus assembled a group of the hardiest mariners he could find. These fellows were so hardy that, had the light bulb been invented at that time, it would have taken at least three of these mariners to screw one in, if you get our drift. On October 8, 1492, they set out across the storm-tossed Atlantic in three tiny ships, the *Ninja,* the *Piña Colada,* and the *Heidy-Ho III.* Fortunately Columbus kept a detailed log, so we can get some sense of how long and arduous their journey was from revealing excerpts such as this:

October 8—Boy, is this journey ever long! Also arduous!

But finally, after numerous storm-tossed weeks, just when it seemed as if Columbus and his men would never see land again, there came an excited cry from the lookout.

"Hey!" he cried. "We forgot to put up the sails!"

And so they all had a hearty laugh, after which
they hoisted the damned things. A few hours later,
on October 8, they came to an island, where Columbus and a convenient interpreter waded ashore
and had the following historic conversation with a
local tribal chief:

> COLUMBUS: You guys are Indians, right?
> TRIBAL CHIEF: K'ham anonoda jawe. ("No. We
>   came over from Asia about twenty thousand
>   years ago via the Land Bridge.")
> COLUMBUS: Listen, we have spent many weeks
>   looking for India in these three storm-tossed,
>   vomit-encrusted ships, and we have cannons
>   pointing at your wigwams, and we say you are
>   Indians.
> TRIBAL CHIEF: B'nomi kawa saki! ("Welcome to
>   India!")

Thus the white men and the Native Americans
were able, through the spirit of goodwill and compromise, to reach the first in what would become a
long series of mutually beneficial, breached agreements that enabled the two cultures to coexist
peacefully for stretches of twenty and sometimes
even thirty days, after which it was usually necessary to negotiate *new* agreements that would be
even *more* mutual and beneficial, until ultimately
the Native Americans were able to perceive the
vast mutual benefits of living in rock-strewn sec-
tors of South Dakota.

THE AGE OF EXPLORATION

When Columbus returned to Spain with the news of his discovery, everybody became very excited and decided to have an Age of Exploration. Immediately, a great many bold adventurers—Magellan, da Gama, de Soto, Chrysler, Picasso, and others—set forth on Voyages of Discovery, only to have their ships bang into each other and sink at the harbor entrance. But they boldly set out again, this time in alphabetical order, and soon they had made some important discoveries, the most important one being that what Columbus had discovered was not India at all, but America, which explained why the inhabitants were called "Native Americans." In Mexico and South America, the Spanish also discovered highly advanced civilizations, which they wisely elected to convert into ruins for use as future tourist attractions.

One of the most famous Spanish explorers was Juan Ponce de León (literally, "John Punched the Lion"), who came to Florida seeking the mythical Fontainebleau Hotel, where, according to legend, if you had one drink, you could have another one for half price on weekdays between 4:00 and 5:30 P.M. He never found it, but he did meet some natives who at first seemed friendly—they gave him a free meal and guided tour of the area—but who then subjected him to a vicious primitive ritual wherein they trapped him in a small room and

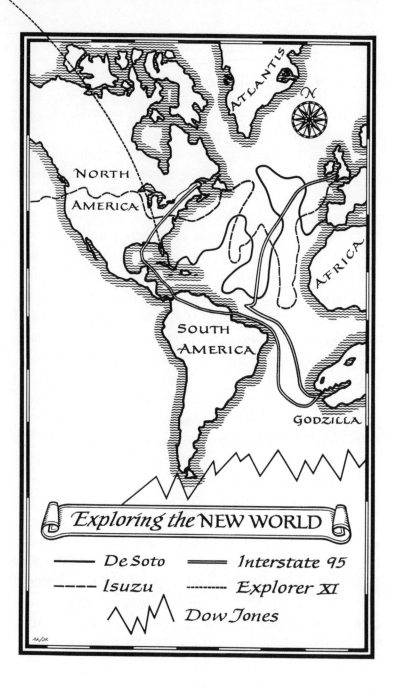

Exploring the NEW WORLD

——— De Soto ═══ Interstate 95

- - - Isuzu ·········· Explorer XI

WWW Dow Jones

repeatedly explained to him the benefits of "time-sharing" in a "vacation resort community" and refused to let him leave, until ultimately he was forced to take his own life.

THE DECLINE OF SPAIN

On October 8, 1565, Spain declined.

DISCUSSION QUESTIONS

1. There's no IRT stop at 104th Street, is there?
2. Did *you* ever purchase time in a time-sharing resort? You *did*? Ha-ha!
3. This question is not technically related to the early Spanish explorations, but we are curious: In the song "Louie Louie," by the Kingsmen, do you think they are singing dirty words? Cite examples.

MAKE A SIMPLE COMPASS

Here's a simple experiment that you might want to try if there is absolutely nothing else going on in your life. All you need is a cork, a bar magnet, and a pail of water. Simply attach your magnet to your cork, then drop it into the water, and *voilà* (literally, "you have a compass")—you have a compass. How does it work? Simple. Notice that, no matter which way you turn the bucket, the cork *always floats on top of the water* (unless the magnet is too heavy). Using this scientific principle, early hardy mariners were able to tell at a glance whether they were sinking!

CHAPTER THREE

England Starts
Some Fun
Colonies

BY THE sixteenth century at approximately 4:30 P.M., England was experiencing a Renaissance. This took the form of Ben Jonson and of course William Shakespeare, the immortal "Barge of Avon," whose plays continue to amuse us to this very day with such hilarious and timely lines as:

> What dost thine flinder knowest of thine face?
> The weg-barrow canst not its row'l misplace![1]

Ha-ha! Whew! Excuse us while we wipe away several tears of helpless laughter! This Golden Age in

[1] From *Antony and Cleopatra IV: Return of the Fungus People,* Act II, Scene iii, seats 103 and 104.

England was called the Elizabethan Era, after the queen, Elizabeth Ann Era, who was known as the "Virgin Queen" because it was not considered a tremendously smart move to call her the "Really Ugly Queen." She inspired many men to leave England on extremely long voyages, which led to expansion.

The first prominent expanding English person was Sir Francis Drake, who, on one of the most famous dates in English history, October 8, defeated the Spanish Armada ("El Armadillo de España"). This was a biggish armada that had ruled the seas for many years, and nobody could defeat it until Sir Francis Drake employed the classic military maneuver of hiding his entire fleet inside a gigantic horse shaped like a Trojan. As you can imagine, this maneuver worked to perfection, and soon the English "ruled the waves," which led to the writing of the hit song[2] "Hail Britannica":

> *Hail Britannica!*
> *Britannica dum de dum.*
> *Dum dum, da de dum dum*
> *Da DEE dum DUM!!*
> (repeat chorus)

[2]and books, a series of twenty-four unopened volumes.

THE ESTABLISHMENT OF THE LOST COLONY

Another English person who existed at around this time was Sir Walter Raleigh, who invented chivalry one day when he encountered the Virgin Queen trying to get across a mud puddle, and he put his cloak over her head. She was very grateful and would have married him immediately, except that he suddenly remembered he had an appointment to sail to North America and found a Lost Colony. He went to an area that he called Virginia, in honor of the fact that it was located next to West Virginia, and he established a colony there, and then—this was the darnedest thing—he lost it. "Think!" his friends would say. "Where did you see it last?" But it was no use, and this particular colony is still missing today. Sometimes you see its picture on milk cartons.

Still, the English were undaunted. "Who the hell needs daunts?" was the English motto in those days. And so a group of merchants decided to start another colony, which they called Jamestown (later known as "Jimtown," and still later, "JimBobtown"), located on an estuary[3] of the Lester A. Hockermeyer, Jr., River. The leader of Jamestown was "John Smith" (not his real name), under whose direction the colony engaged in a number of activities, primarily related to starving. They also managed to form the first

[3] A person who works for an insurance company.

primitive corporation, and, despite the fact that they lacked food and clothing and housing, they courageously engaged in various corporate activities. They would lie around in the snow, dictating primitive memoranda to each other about the need to look into the feasibility of forming a committee to examine the various long-term benefits and drawbacks of maybe planting some corn. Somehow, they managed to survive those first few harsh years, although at one point they were forced to eat their own appointment calendars.

There is an old Virginia saying that goes: "The darkest part of the tunnel is always just before the tollbooth." And this indeed turned out to be true, for just when the Jamestown colonists were about to give up, they came up with a promising new product concept: tobacco. With remarkable foresight, these early executives recognized that there was a vast untapped market for a product that consumers could set on fire and inhale so as to gradually turn their lungs into malignant lumps of carbon. Soon the Jamestown colony was shipping tons of tobacco back to England, and had even begun to develop primitive advertising campaigns featuring pictures of rugged men on horseback and slogans such as:

SMOKE TOBACCO
"It won't gradually turn your lungs
into malignant lumps of carbon!"

Although of course there have been many scientific advances in advertising, such as having the rugged men ride in helicopters, this basic message remains in use to this very day.

Another concept that was in the early stages of development in Virginia was democracy. By 1619, a rudimentary legislature had formed, and several years later it had mutated into two houses, called "the upper house" and "Steve." For a bill to become law, it had to be passed by a two-thirds majority of both houses, after which it was sent back to the king, James II, who would tear it into pieces the size of postage stamps and feed them to his dog, Bart XI. So it was not *total* democracy as we know it today, but it was a start.

Yet all was not well. Because at the same time the clouds of religious intolerance, propelled by a large arctic air mass of hatred, were forming a major storm front of persecution, which was to result in one of the most moving stories of courage and faith in all of American history, not to mention a four-day weekend. We refer, of course, to the Puritans.

THE STORY
OF THE PURITANS

The Puritans were an extremely religious group who lived in England and did not believe in drinking or dancing or having sex with hooved animals. They were very unpopular. So they decided to sail over to the New World, where they would be free to worship as they chose and live in peace and harmony and set fire to suspected witches.

And thus it was that in some specific year, the Puritans, taking with them little more than stupid hats and an unwavering faith in Providence,[4] set sail across the dark and treacherous North Atlantic in the *Mayflower*, a cramped, frail ship of Panamanian registry. The crossing was brutally harsh. Only two days out of port, a fierce storm destroyed most of the shuffleboard equipment. As giant waves washed over their tiny ship, tossing it about like a cork, the Puritans, realizing their fate was not in their own hands, got down on their knees and, drawing on some inner strength, threw up. Then they looked toward the heavens and vowed that if, by some miracle, they were able to make it safely to their destination, they were definitely going to get a new travel agent.

Finally, just when the Puritans were starting to think that maybe drinking and dancing wouldn't be so bad after all, the lookout spotted the coast of Massachusetts. This resulted in a tremendous hue and of course cry aboard the ship as the Puritans rushed excitedly up on deck and shoved the navigator overboard, because he was supposed to be aiming for Virginia.

By that point, however, the *Mayflower*, which

[4] A city in Rhode Island that, unbeknownst to the Puritans, had not been founded yet.

had no shower facilities, was starting to smell like the postgame laundry hamper of a professional ice-hockey team, so the Puritans decided to row ashore and land at Plymouth Rock.[5] But first, for insurance purposes, they all had to sign the Mayflower Compact. This was a historic document that set forth what would become some of our most fundamental and cherished principles of government, as is shown by this direct quotation:

6. No spitting on the sidewalk.

When the Puritans landed, they found themselves in a harsh and desolate world, and they probably would have starved to death if not for the help of a friendly local Native American named Squanto.[6] Squanto looked at the Puritans barging around the wilderness with their hats and their comical Puritan muskets shaped like trombones at the end, and he took pity on them. "Look," he said, because fortunately he spoke English, "what you need to do is plant some corn." And so they did, and after a couple of months it grew and ripened, and the Puritans, who by this time were hungrier than ever, boiled it and ate it with butter and a little salt. "Next time, you should try shucking it first," advised Squanto.

Eventually, as you would expect, a year went

[5]So called because it is shaped like a Plymouth.
[6]Meaning "Native American."

by. The Puritans decided that, all things considered, it had been a pretty good year, except for the fact that the vast majority of them were at that point dead, so they decided to have the first traditional Thanksgiving. They invited Squanto over to join them in eating a turkey ("Next time," advised the ever-helpful Squanto, "try cooking it first"), after which they watched the Lions-Bears game. Then the Puritans told Squanto that they were very grateful for all he had done, but that frankly they would not be needing him anymore, so he and his tribe should go find some other area to be natives of. In the next several years the Puritans became prosperous and built New England, parts of which can still be seen today.

DISCUSSION QUESTIONS

1. Why only hooved animals?
2. Did any of your ancestors come over on the *Mayflower*? So what?
3. If you were on the Detroit Lions, would you be ticked off about always having to play on Thanksgiving? Explain.

CHAPTER FOUR

The Colonies Develop a Life-style

THE TYPICAL life-style in the early colonies was very harsh. There was no such thing as the modern supermarket, which meant that the hardy colonists had to get up before dawn and spend many hours engaging in tedious tasks such as churning butter. They would put some butter in a churn, and they would whack it with a pole for several hours, and then they'd mop their brows and say, "Why the hell don't we get a modern supermarket around here!" And then, because it was illegal to curse, they would be forced to stand in the stocks while the first tourists took pictures of them.

So it was harsh, all right, but nevertheless more and more persecuted religious minorities—Protestants, Catholics, Jews, Scientologists, Cubs fans— were flocking to freedom and establishing religious colonies such as Maryland and Heritage Village, USA, site of the New World's first known Christian water slide.

THE ENGLAND-HOLLAND RIVALRY

Meanwhile, England got into a rivalry with Holland. Although today Holland is known primarily for being underwater and making Heineken beer, in those days it claimed a great deal of land in the New World because of the important explorations of the brave Dutch explorer for whom the Hudson River is named, Henry Hudson River.[1] Based on these explorations, Holland claimed all of the land west of the Atlantic Ocean and north of the equator. This angered the English, who claimed all of the land in the world and a substantial section of Mars, and so on October 8 a rivalry broke out between the two nations.

The largest Dutch settlement at the time was New Amsterdam, located on the site of what is now New York City and which had established a thriving economy based on illegal parking. So one day an English individual named James "Duke of" York sailed into the harbor with his fleet and captured New Amsterdam without the Dutch firing a single shot. He was able to do this because at

[1] He should have been in Chapter Two, but we forgot.

the time the city's commissioner for the Department of Firing Back was testifying before the Special Grand Jury to Investigate Municipal Corruption, which is still in session. And thus was the name of New Amsterdam changed to "The Big Apple."

Meanwhile, more colonists were arriving, a good example being William Penn, who founded the colony that still bears his name, New Jersey. But life in the New World continued to be harsh, with most colonists leading a hand-to-mouth existence. "Take your hand out of your mouth!" their mothers were always shouting, but you know how it is with colonists. What they really needed, to get themselves off their duffs, was for trade to develop. Luckily, several days later this occurred.

THE DEVELOPMENT OF TRADE

One morning the colonists noticed that the New World contained a number of products that were not available in Europe, such as turpentine, which could easily be obtained in the colonies simply by boiling trees. Soon the colonists were sending barrels of turpentine across to England, where the English people would dump it on the ground, because, let's face it, a little turpentine goes a long way. Then the English people would fill the boat up with some product *they* had a surplus of, such as used snuff, and they'd send it back to the colonies; and then the colonists would retaliate with, say, barrels of dirt, and so on, until trade had escalated to the point where the two sides were sending entire boatloads of diseased rats back and forth.

But life was not all hard work in the colonies. Culture was also starting to rear its head, in the form of the Early American Novel. The most famous novelist of this era was Cliff, the author of the famous *Cliff Notes,* a series of works that are still immensely popular with high school students. The best known, of course, is *The Scarlet Ladder,* which tells the story of a short man named Miles Standish, who lived in a tall house with seven people named Gable, only to be killed in a sled crash with an enormous white whale. This was to become a recurring theme in colonial literature.

But little did the colonists realize, as these cultural and economic developments were taking place, that they were about to become involved in friction with the French. The cause of this was . . . Hold it! We have just received the following:

EDUCATIONAL ADVISORY ALERT

A REVIEW COMMITTEE CONSISTING OF EDUCATION PROFESSIONALS WITH DOCTORATE DEGREES AND INITIALS AFTER THEIR NAMES HAS DETERMINED THAT, SO FAR, THIS HISTORY BOOK IS NOT MAKING ENOUGH OF AN EFFORT TO INCLUDE THE CONTRIBUTIONS OF WOMEN AND MINORITY GROUPS. UNLESS SOME EFFORT IS UNDERTAKEN TO CORRECT THIS SITUATION, THIS BOOK WILL NOT BE APPROVED FOR PURCHASE BY PUBLIC SCHOOL SYSTEMS IN ABSOLUTELY VAST QUANTITIES.

Another important fact we just now remembered is that during the colonial era women and minority groups were making many contributions, which we are certain that they will continue to do at regularly spaced intervals throughout the course of this book. But right now, let's get back to:

FRICTION WITH THE FRENCH

French traders came to the northern part of the New World to barter with the Native Americans for their pelts of beavers, minks, otters, elks, muskellunges, and so forth. The two sides quickly learned to communicate with each other using a stripped-down bartering language, as shown by this painstakingly researched historical re-creation:

FRENCH TRADER: How does this look?
NATIVE AMERICAN: Honey, that pelt is *you*!
FRENCH TRADER: Really, Red? You don't think it's too bunched at the hips?
NATIVE AMERICAN: Listen, bunched at the hips is *the* look in the New World.
FRENCH TRADER: I'll take it!

Soon the French, aided by Native American guides, were penetrating deep into North America in search of matching belts, shoes, and other accessories. By the late seventeenth century, pioneering

French designers such as Marquette and Joliet (most of them went by only one name) had made a number of major fashion advances in the New World. The basis of the entire French colonial philosophy was natural fibers, in stark contrast to the British, who were already using water-driven looms to make primitive polyesters. It was only a matter of time before friction broke out in the form of:

The French and Indian War

The French and Indian War is highly significant because, as David Boldt[2] points out, it had a stupid name. It sounded like the French were fighting the *Indians,* whereas in fact they were supposed to be on the same side. The British didn't even realize they were supposed to be *in* this war until several years after it started, by which time the French and the Indians, totally confused, had inflicted heavy casualties upon each other. So England won the war, and on October 8 the French king, Louis the Somethingth, signed the Treaty of Giving Away Canada, under which he gave away Canada. *"Que l'enfer,"* he remarked at the time, *"c'est seulement Canada."*[3]

[2]A friend of ours. You don't know him.
[3]"What the hell, it's only Canada."

DISCUSSION QUESTIONS

1. How come, if the country is called "Holland," the people are called "Dutch"?
2. Have you ever noticed that on those rare occasions when you *do* need turpentine, the can, which you bought in 1978 and have been moving from household to household ever since, is always empty?
3. Do you feel that people who insist upon referring to themselves as "doctor" simply because they hold Ph.D. degrees, which are about as rare as air molecules, tend to be self-important weenies? And what about the use of the word "professional," as in "automotive sales professional"? Does that make you want to puke, or what? Explain.

CHAPTER FIVE

The Birthing Contractions of a Nation

WHAT CAUSED the American Revolution? This is indeed a rhetorical question that for many years historians have begun chapters with. As well they should. For the American Revolution is without doubt the single most important historical event ever to occur in this nation except of course for Super Bowl III.[1]

One big causal factor in the Revolution was that England operated under what political scientists describe as "The Insane Venereally Diseased Hunchbacked Homicidal King" system of government. This basically means that for some reason, again possibly the food, the English king always

[1] Jets 16, Colts 7. This historian won $35.

turned out to be a syphilitic hunchbacked lunatic
whose basic solution to virtually all problems, including humidity, was to have somebody's head
cut off. There was one king, Henry "Henry the
Eighth" VIII, who could barely get through a
day without beheading a wife. It reached the
point, with Henry, where the clergyman had dif-
ficulty completing the wedding ceremony:

> CLERGYMAN: I now pronounce you man and . . .
> WATCH OUT! (SLICE)

This style of government was extremely expen-
sive, especially in terms of dry-cleaning costs, and
as a result the kings were always trying to raise
money from the colonies by means of taxation.
This was bad enough without representation, but
what really ticked the colonists off were the tax
forms, which were extremely complicated, as is
shown by this actual example:

> To determineth the amounteth that thou canst
> claimeth for depreciation to thine cow, deducteth
> the amount showneth on Line XVLIICX-A of
> Schedule XIV, from the amount showneth on
> Line CVXILIIVMM of Schedule XVVII . . . No,
> waiteth, we meaneth Line XCII of Schedule
> CXVIILMM . . . No, holdeth it, we meaneth . . .

And so on. In 1762 the king attempted to respond
to the colonists' concerns by setting up a special
Taxpayer Assistance Service, under which colo-

nist with questions about their tax returns could get on a special toll-free ship and sail to England, where specially trained Tax Assistors would beat them to death with sticks. But even that failed to satisfy the more radical colonists, and it soon became clear that within a short time—possibly even in the next page—the situation would turn ugly.

THE SITUATION TURNS UGLY

One afternoon some freedom-loving colonists known as the Boston Patriots were sitting around their locker room, trying to think up ways to throw off the yoke of colonial oppression. Suddenly one of them, Bob, had an idea:

"Hey!" he said. "Let's dress up like the locals and throw tea into the harbor!"

Instantly the other Patriots were galvanized. "What was that?" they shouted.

"A galvanic reaction," responded Bob. "Named for the Italian physiologist Luigi Galvani (1737–1798), who conducted experiments wherein he sent electrical currents through the legs of frogs."

But the Boston Patriots were not the only people engaging in inhumane scientific research during the colonial era. Another person doing this was Benjamin Franklin, who, in a famous experiment, sought to prove his theory that if you flew a kite in a rainstorm, a huge chunk of electricity would come shooting down the string and damage your brain. Sure enough, he was right, and he spent the rest of his days making bizarre, useless, and unintelligible statements such as: "A penny saved is a penny earned." Eventually he became so dodderingly pathetic that he had to be placed in charge of the U.S. Postal Service. Also around this time women and minority groups were accomplishing a great many achievements.

But getting back to the Boston Patriots: Later that night, they boldly carried out Bob's bold plan of dressing up as Native Americans and throwing tea into the harbor, but for some reason this did not result in Independence. "Maybe we should also toss in some lemon," somebody suggested. And so they did this, and then they tried some Sweet 'n Low; still no sign of Independence. Also the harbor was starting to look like a toxic-waste dump, which did not go unnoticed by early ancestors of future president George Herbert Walker Piedmont Harrington Armoire Vestibule Bush.

This angered the king, so he ordered Parliament to pass the Stamp Act, under which every time the colonists made a purchase, the cashier would give them some stamps, and they had to paste these into books, which was even more boring than churning butter. When the colonists had acquired a certain number of stamps, they were required to go down to the Royal Stamp Redemption Center and exchange them for cheap cookware (£4.5 million) or tacky folding card tables (£3 billion). As you can imagine, this was less than popular with the colonists, whose anger was eloquently expressed by Tom Paine in his fiery pamphlet *Common Sense,* which, in its most famous passage, states: "How many fondue sets does any one colonial family *need*?"

This further enraged the king, who, as you have probably gathered by now, had the political savvy of a croissant. He ordered Parliament to pass the Irritation Acts, whose entire purpose was to make life in the colonies even *more* miserable. These included:

1. *The Sneeze Shield Act,* requiring that all colonial salad bars had to have shields suspended over them—allegedly for "sanitary" purposes, but actually intended to make it difficult for short colonists to reach the chick-peas.
2. *The Pill Blockade Act,* requiring that colonial aspirin bottles had to come with wads of cotton stuffed in the top, making the aspirin virtually inaccessible, especially to colonists with hangovers.
3. *The Eternal Container Act,* requiring that colonists who purchased appliances had to save the original packing cartons forever and ever, passing them down through the generations, or else they would void their warranties.

All of these factors caused the tension in the colonies to mount with each passing day, as can been seen from the following chart:

LEVEL OF COLONIAL TENSION

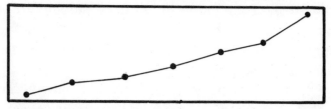

MON   TUE   WED   THU   FRI   SAT   SUN

It was amid this climate of rising tension and anger, with a 50 percent chance of lingering afternoon and evening violence, that the First Continental Congress was held. It met in Philadelphia, and its members, realizing that the actions they took in this hour of crisis could very well determine the fate of the New World, voted, after many hours of angry debate, to give themselves a pay raise. There was no turning back now. Clearly, the stage had been set for the Discussion Questions.

DISCUSSION QUESTIONS

1. Do you think Unitas should have started for the Colts?
2. What the hell *are* chick-peas, anyway?

CHAPTER SIX

Kicking Some British Butt

THE Revolutionary War began with the famous Midnight Ride of Paul Revere, immortalized in the well-known verse:

> *Out of the bed and onto the floor;*
> *Fifty-yard dash to the bathroom door!*

Whoops! Our mistake. This verse comes from the famous song "Midnight Attack of Diarrhea," which used to absolutely slay us when we were campers at Camp Sharparoon.[1] The Midnight Ride of Paul Revere is also very inspirational. By day, Revere was a Boston silversmith,[2] but by

---

[1] 1953–1956.
[2] A person who smithed silver.

night, like so many patriots during the Revolutionary era, he had insomnia. He would lie awake, tossing and turning, until finally one night, irritated by lights that somebody kept shining in his window from the Old North Church, he just flipped out. He leaped onto his horse and raced off into the night, shrieking. This infuriated a group of British soldiers, who marched out after him, but they, too, were noisy, because in those days—remember, this was literally centuries before the discovery of the Rolling Stones—the British had a terrible sense of rhythm (they were mostly white guys) and could march only with the aid of drums.

So what would happen is, Paul Revere would come shrieking through a picturesque slumbering New England town at 2:30 A.M., and the townspeople, who were already uptight because of the mounting tension described previously, would come rushing out in their pajamas, really ticked off, and the first thing they'd see were these British soldiers barging down the street, whanging on their drums as though it were halftime at the Rose Bowl, and as you can imagine it was not long before violence erupted in the form of the Battle of Lexington.

Battles in those days took longer than they do today. First off, it took a while for the British to form into strict military formations, which, when viewed from the air, spelled out nationalistic slogans such as GO BRITS! This delay caused a great deal of irritation among the patriots:

PATRIOTS: C'mon! Aren't you guys ready *yet*??
BRITISH: Not yet! Say, can you chaps give us a hand? We need two more men to cross the "T."

Another problem was that the guns they used in those days, called muskets, took forever to load. First you had to put your powder in, then you had to put in a little piece of flint, then you had to ram some wadding down there, then you had to put in about a quarter teaspoon of paprika, and finally you had to put in your musket ball, which usually popped right back out again because there was hardly any room. It took so long to complete the Battle of Lexington that the two sides were nearly four hours late to the next scheduled event, the Battle of Concord. This was where the Americans invented the innovative guerrilla tactic of rushing up to the British, who were still dithering around with their formation ("Dammit, Nigel! You're supposed to be part of the 'O'!"), and bonking them manually over the heads with their unloaded muskets.

And thus the first round of the Revolutionary War went to the rebels. But Independence was not to be bought cheaply, for soon the king was sending reinforcements, seasoned troops who could form not only words, but also a locomotive with moving wheels. The rebels, realizing that they were in for a long, hard fight, decided to form the *Second* Continental Congress, whose members voted, after a long and stormy session, to grant themselves only a cost-of-living increase.

But this Continental Congress also knew that they would need an army, and they knew just the man to lead it—a man who was universally respected and admired, a man who had the experience and leadership needed to organize troops and lead them into battle. That man, of course, was: Dwight Eisenhower. Unfortunately, he would not be born for at least another dozen chapters, so they decided to go with George Washington, known as "The Father of His Country" because of such exploits as throwing a cherry bomb across the Potomac.

As leader of the American forces, Washington faced a most difficult task, because the Continental Army was poorly equipped. Just to cite one example, it had no soldiers. When Washington wanted to do the "Cadence Count" marching song, he would have to do both the "Sound off!" and the "One! Two!" part.

Eventually, however, Washington was able to recruit some troops via a promotion wherein if you enlisted in the army, you and a friend got an all-expenses-paid Winter for Two at Valley Forge. Nonetheless, the American troops were poor and ill trained. Many of them wore rags on their feet. They also wore their shoes on their heads. These were not exactly nuclear physicists, if you sense our meaning. But they were patriotic men, and they had a secret weapon that the king had not bargained on: "Yankee Doodle." This was the Official Theme Song of the American Revolution, and when the Americans marched into battle singing the inspirational part about how Yankee Doodle "stuck a feather in his cap and called it macaroni," the effect on the British troops was devastating. "He called it *what*?" they would ask each other in confusion, thus giving the Americans the opening they needed to rush up and whack them with muskets.

This forced the king to try a new ploy: He sent over the Hessians, who spoke no English and consequently paid little attention to "Yankee Doodle." That was the good news for the British side. The bad news was, the Hessians were actually German, which meant that the words they formed in their battle formations were humongous. For example, their equivalent of GO BRITS! was: WANN-FAHRTDERSUGAB EIN UMWIEVIELUHRKOMMTERAN! It would sometimes take them days to form a simple preposition.

Meanwhile, in Philadelphia, the Continental Congress, in an atmosphere of crisis, was trying to write the Declaration of Independence. The responsibility for this task had originally been assigned to the Special Joint Committee for Writing the Declaration of Independence, whose members immediately voted to go on a fact-finding mission,

with their spouses, to the French Riviera. It soon
became clear that it was going to take them a long
time just to declare their souvenir purchases, let
alone independence, so the task fell to Thomas
Jefferson. On a historic night in 1776, the lanky
red-haired Virginian picked up a quill pen and
began scratching on a historic piece of parchment.
He worked all night, and by morning he was ready
to show his results to the others.

"Aren't you supposed to dip the pen into the
ink?" the others asked.

And so the lanky red-haired Virginian went
back to work for another historic night, and by
dawn he had produced the document that has
come to express the ideals and hopes and dreams
of an entire nation.

THE DECLARATION OF INDEPENDENCE

When, in the course of human events, it becomes
necessary for one people to dissolve the political
bands which have connected them with another,
and to assume among the powers of the earth the
separate and equal station to which the laws of
nature and of nature's God entitle them, a decent
respect to the opinions of mankind require that
they should get some sleep. Because I have been
up for two nights now, declaring independence,
and I may be a lanky Virginian but I am not a
machine, for heaven's sake, and it just doesn't
make sense to sit here scrawling away these com-
pound-complex sentences when I just know nobody's going to read them, because nobody ever

does read all the way through these legal documents. Take leases. You take the average tenants, and you could put a lease in front of them with a clause about halfway through stating that they have to eat toasted moose doots for breakfast, and I guarantee you they'll never read it. Not that it would make any difference if they did, because tenants ignore most of the rules anyway, such as the rules about not flushing inappropriate objects down the toilet. Ask any landlord what he spends most of his time doing, and the odds are he'll answer, "Pulling inappropriate objects out of tenants' toilets." I know one landlord who found a gerbil in there. Who the hell would do a thing like that? A cat, yes. I could see that. I could see giving a modest *rebate* for that. But not a gerbil. I gotta lie down.

The members of the Continental Congress were extremely impressed by what Jefferson had written, at least the part that they read, and on the following day, October 8, the nation celebrated its very first July Fourth. The members took turns lighting sparklers and signing their John Hancocks to the Declaration, with one prankster even going so far as to actually write "John Hancock." But soon it was time for the Congress to return to the serious business at hand: issuing press releases.

Meanwhile, women and minority groups were making many important contributions. So were the French, who supported the patriot cause and sent over many invaluable fashion hints. But still the American troops were badly outnumbered, and they probably would never have won if not for the occurrence of:

THE TURNING POINT

This turning point occurred in Trenton, New Jersey, where the Hessians had decided to spend Christmas, which should give you an idea of how out of it *they* were. As night fell, they got to drinking heavily and singing "Ninety-nine Bottles of Beer on the Wall," which takes forever in German, so it was the ideal time for the Americans to attack. Unfortunately, the ice-infested Delaware River lay between the two armies. The situation looked bleak, and all eyes turned to George Washington.

"We'll row over there in boats," he said, displaying the kind of leadership that he was famous for.

And so they climbed into some boats, and, after pausing briefly to pose for a famous oil painting by Emanuel Leutze,[3] they captured Trenton while suffering virtually no casualties, although a number of them did get urinated on. It was a major victory for the Americans.

But the Revolutionary War was not over yet. No, the historic Treaty of Ending the Revolutionary War was not to be signed for five more long

[3] 1816–1868.

years, years of pain, years of sacrifice, and—above all—years that will not be included in this book, because at the rate we're going through history here, we're never even going to get to the Civil War.

DISCUSSION QUESTIONS

1. Have you ever flushed anything inappropriate down a toilet? Explain.
2. How come, in the famous oil painting by Emanuel Leutze, it looks like George Washington has a group the size of the Mormon Tabernacle Choir in his rowboat?
3. Whatever happened to the Hessians, anyway? You never see them around.

CHAPTER SEVEN

The Forging of a Large, Wasteful Bureaucracy

AGAINST ALL ODDS, the colonists had won the war against England; now they faced an even greater task: planning the victory party. Who should be invited? Where would they put their coats? These were just two of the questions confronting the leaders of the fledgling nation. Also, extreme factions in several states felt that there should be some kind of government.

And so the leading statespersons from all thirteen states gathered in Philadelphia for a Constitutional Convention. There, over the bitter objections of conservatives, they voted to approve the historic Fashion Statement of 1787, under which delegates were required to wear knee pants, tight stockings, and wigs accessorized with ribbons. It was a radical pronouncement, and the delegates paid a high price for it—nearly half had to purchase completely new wardrobes. The convention had established that the old way of doing things was not going to be acceptable, which meant that they also had to come up with a bold new designer look for the government.

But there was much disagreement among the delegates about exactly what this look should be. Some wanted a weak president and a strong legislature. Some wanted a smart president and a dumb legislature. Some wanted a very short president and a deaf legislature. The New York delegation, typically, wanted a loud president and a rude legislature. Day after day the delegates argued, but they seemed to be getting no closer to agreement, and the new nation was in danger of collapsing before it ever really had a chance to get started. But just when the convention appeared to be at a total impasse, the aging statesman Benjamin Franklin rose to his feet and, as the other delegates listened raptly, emitted a three-foot streamer of drool. The others alertly took this to be a sign from the wily veteran communicator that it was time to ratify the U.S. Constitution, and so they did.

THE U.S. CONSTITUTION

The Constitution divides the federal government into three equal branches:

1. Mammoth, labyrinthian departments set up for purposes that no individual taxpayer would ever in a million years voluntarily spend money on.
2. Mammoth, labyrinthian departments set up for purposes that probably made a lot of sense originally, but nobody can remember what they are.
3. Statuary.

This separation of powers creates a system of "checks and balances," which protects everybody by ensuring that any action taken by one part of the government will be rendered utterly meaningless by an equal and opposite reaction from some other part.

The highest-ranking officer in the government is the president, who is elected to a four-year term after a three-year, nine-month campaign in which he is required to state that he has a Vision and plans to provide Leadership. The president's primary duties are to get on helicopters; bitch about Congress; and send the vice president abroad to frown with sorrow at the remains of deceased foreign leaders.

The Constitution also provides for the election of a Senate, which consists of two white men in gray suits from each state; and a House of Representatives, which consists of three or four hundred men named "Bob" or "Dick" with blond wives whose hobbies are gardening, furniture, and the mentally retarded. The primary duties of the members of both houses of Congress are:

1. Running for reelection.
2. Having staffs.
3. Getting subsidized haircuts.
4. Sending out newsletters featuring photographs of themselves standing next to the president, designed to create the impression that the president is relying upon them for advice and counsel, when he is in fact trying to remember who the hell they are.

How a Bill Becomes a Law

First the bill secretes a substance that it uses to form a cocoon, and then it . . . No, sorry. That's how a caterpillar becomes a butterfly. The way a bill becomes a law is:

1. A member of Congress notices that there is some problem afflicting the nation. For example, he might notice that the nation is not observing a sufficient quantity of idiot official days and weeks, such as National Tractor Mechanic Awareness Week, and so he introduces a bill to correct this problem.
2. The bill is referred to a committee, which forms a subcommittee for the purpose of going to Geneva, Switzerland, to see if there are any facts there that might be useful.
3. The bill is reported back to the committee, which holds hearings and receives testimony

from interested parties such as the American Aspirin Bottle Manufacturers Association.

4. Needed amendments are attached to the bill, for example an amendment designed to protect the American consumer from the potential dangers of aspirin bottles manufactured by unfair foreign competitors.
5. The bill is reported out of the committee.
6. Everybody goes on vacation for a couple of weeks.
7. The bill is reported back to the committee.
8. The bill is reported to the police.
9. The Supreme Court declares the bill to be unconstitutional.
10. The Cheese stands alone.

The Bill of Rights

The first ten amendments to the Constitution are known as "The Bill of Rights," because that is what everybody calls them. These amendments spell out the basic rights that all of us enjoy as Americans:

- *The First Amendment* states that members of religious groups, no matter how small or unpopular, shall have the right to hassle you in airports.
- *The Second Amendment* states that, since a well-regulated militia is necessary to the security of a free state, you can buy high-powered guns via mail order and go out into the woods with your friends and absolutely vaporize some deer.

- *The Third Amendment* states that you don't have to quarter troops inside your house. "You troops are just going to have to sleep on the patio" is a perfectly constitutional thing for you to tell them.
- *The Fourth Amendment* states that if your aunt had testicles, she would be your uncle.
- *The Fifth Amendment* states that your Fifth Amendment rights cannot be violated until you are advised of them.
- *The Sixth Amendment* states that if you are accused of a crime, you have the right to a trial before a jury of people too stupid to get out of jury duty.
- *The Seventh Amendment* states that if you are in the Express Lane, and you have more than one item of produce of the same biological type, such as two grapefruit, you have the right to count these as one item in order to keep yourself under the ten-item limit.
- *The Eighth Amendment* states that if you are seated directly in front of a person who has to comment on every single scene in the movie— and we are talking here about *perceptive* comments, such as when a movie character is getting into his car and the person behind you says, "He's getting into his car now"—then you have the right to go "SSSHHHHH!" two times in a warning manner, after which you have the right to kill this person with a stick.
- *The Ninth Amendment* states that you shall not covet your neighbor's wife.
- *The Tenth Amendment* states that, OK, if your neighbor's wife is dropping a lot of hints, really coming *on* to you, that is a different matter.

Ratification of the Constitution

It took a long time for the states to ratify the Constitution, because in those days communication was difficult. After a state legislature had voted for ratification, a messenger would be dispatched on horseback to carry the word to the new nation's capital. Often he would ride for days over poor roads through sparsely populated wilderness areas until he realized that the new nation *had* no capital. "Ha-ha!" he would remark to his horse. "That darned legislature has tricked me again!" Then he would be attacked by bears. Clearly a capital was needed. The logical choice seemed to be Washington, D.C., a city blessed with a natural beltway teeming with consultants.

Also we should keep in mind that women and minority groups were continuing to make some gigantic contributions.

THE ELECTION OF THE FIRST PRESIDENT

The leading contender in the first presidential election race was George Washington, who waged a campaign based on heavy exposure in media such as coins, stamps, and famous oil paintings. This shrewd strategy carried him to a landslide victory in which he carried every state except Massachusetts, which voted for George McGovern.

And thus it was that on October 8, the newly

sworn-in president stood before a large cheering throng of his fellow countrymen and delivered his famous inaugural address, in which he offered the famous stirring words "We cannot [something] the [machines? birds?] of [something] will never [something]. As far as I know." Unfortunately, there were no microphones back then. This was only one of the problems facing the fledgling nation, as we shall see.

DISCUSSION QUESTIONS

1. How come history books never have sex scenes? You know, like: "James Madison, unable to restrain his passion any longer, thrust his ink-engorged pen into the second draft of the *Federalist Papers.*"
2. Scientists tell us that the fastest animal on earth, with a top speed of 120 feet per second, is a cow that has been dropped out of a helicopter. How long, traveling at top speed, will it take the cow to travel 360 feet?

CHAPTER EIGHT

A Brash Young Nation Gets into Wars and Stuff

ONCE THE federal government was organized, the biggest problem was how to pay off the fledgling nation's massive war debt. The Founding Fathers were starting to get disturbing letters like this:

Dear Mr. Father:

This is the fourth time we've written regarding your outstanding balance of $23,784,982.34. While we certainly value your fledgling business, we must inform you that unless you immediately make arrangements to repay this amount, we will regretfully have to return you to British rule.

Sincerely,
The VISA Corporation
"More Powerful than God"

Fortunately, one of the Founding Fathers was a shrewd financial thinker named Alexander Hamilton, who came up with an idea for repayment of the debt based on a concept so brilliant—and yet so simple—that it remains extremely popular with governments to this very day.

"Let's print money with our pictures on it," Hamilton suggested.

And so they did. The hardest part was deciding which Founding Father would get to be on which denomination of bill, an issue that led to the infamous duel between Hamilton and Aaron Burr, both of whom wanted to be on the fifty. Burr won the duel in overtime, although years later he died anyway, little realizing that his great-great-grandson Raymond Burr would go on to become one of the widest actors in American history.

THE ELECTION OF 1792

George Washington decided to run for reelection in 1792, because he felt that his work was not finished. In fact, it wasn't even started, because, the roads being what they were, he had spent his entire first term en route from his Virginia home to the temporary U.S. capital in Philadelphia. His slogan was:

VOTE FOR GEORGE WASHINGTON
"He's Almost As Far As Baltimore."

Washington was reelected unanimously and reached Philadelphia several months later, only to learn that the capital was now operating out of Washington, D.C., which he managed to reach just in time to deliver his famous farewell address, containing the prophetic warning "We should get [something] has to [something] these darned [something] complex all over the place."

THE RISE OF POLITICAL PARTIES

With Washington no longer on the scene, political parties began to form, the main ones being the Republicans, the Federalists, the Sharks, the Home Boys, the Del-Vikings, and the Church of Scientology. The major issue dividing these parties was whether the United States should enter into an alliance with France in its war with Britain. It was not an easy decision: On the one hand, France had provided invaluable support during the Revolutionary War, support without which the colonies might never have achieved their independence from the brutal tyranny of England; on the other hand, France contained a lot of French people. You tried to form an alliance with them, and all they did was smirk at your pronunciation. Ultimately a compromise was reached under which the United States signed a treaty with brutal, tyrannical old England, and sent the wily veteran diplomat Benjamin Franklin over to mollify France with a nice basket of apples, which he ate en route.

In 1796 John Adams was elected as the nation's second president, thanks to the support of the Anal Compulsive Party, whose members believed that henceforth presidents should be elected in alphabetical order so that it would be easier to remember them all during history tests. It was during Adams's administration that the famous "XYZ Affair" took place. What happened was, Adams sent a diplomatic mission over to France to protest the fact that the French were seizing American ships and redecorating them by force. When the Americans got to France, the French foreign minister told them to meet with three secret agents, known only as "X," "Y," and "Z."

"If you can guess their real names and occupations," the French foreign minister said, "you'll receive diplomatic recognition *and* the Brunswick pool table!"

Unfortunately the Americans could correctly identify only one agent[1] and never reached the bonus round, but they did receive some lovely consolation prizes.

Another major event to occur around this time was the passage of the Alien and Sedition Acts, which made it illegal to engage in acts of sedition with an alien unless you were both consenting adults. This so enraged the voters that they elected Thomas Jefferson as the third president,

[1]Kitty Carlisle.

thus ruining the alphabetical-order concept and plunging the nation into what historians refer to as the Era of Presidents Whose Names Nobody Can Remember, which did not end until President Evelyn Lincoln.

But this did not stop women and minority groups from continuing to achieve many noteworthy achievements.

Meanwhile, Jefferson faced the issue of what to do about the Barbary States, a group of small pirate nations on the Mediterranean that were preying on international commerce by sailing out to passing merchant ships and demanding spare change. Most major nations were paying bribes, or "tribute," to the Barbary States in exchange for safe passage, but Jefferson angrily rejected this idea with his famous epigram "The hell with those dirtbags."

So he sent some warships over there to explain to the pirates, in diplomatic terms, the various international diplomatic implications of having their bodies perforated by eight-inch cannonball holes, and the pirates agreed to cool it. This bold action by Jefferson established an honorable American tradition of "getting tough" with terrorists that continued in the United States until the latter half of the twentieth century, when it was replaced by the tradition of "calling a press conference and threatening to get tough" with terrorists.

THE LOUISIANA PURCHASE

While this was going on, England and France were at war with Spain. Or perhaps England and Spain were at war with ... No! This is it: France and Spain were at war with England. But only because Germany did not exist at the time. As far as we know.

Anyway, the result was that for some reason France decided to sell a large piece of property in North America. The French government put the following advertisement in *The New York Times* real estate section:

NICE PIECE OF LAND approx. 34 hillion jillion acres convenient to West perfect for growing nation.

So Jefferson did a little checking and he found that this property was in fact zoned for Westward Expansion, and he made an offer of $12 million. The French countered with $15 million, but they also threw in the appliances, and they had themselves a deal. After the closing ceremony, Jefferson sent Lewis and Clark off to hold the Lewis and Clark Expedition. It was hard going: The land was wild and untamed; there were hostile Americans around; and Clark bitched constantly because he thought it should be called "The Clark and Lewis Expedition." Nevertheless, they were able to explore the entire region, and when they returned to Washington on October 8 they reported that it contained not just Louisiana; but a whole bunch of other states as well, although some of them, such as South Dakota, needed work.

Meanwhile, in Europe, the situation worsened as England joined France in declaring war against Spain, unaware that France had joined Spain in declaring war against England, and that Spain, acting in haste, had accidentally declared war against itself. The United States tried, by depressing the clutch of diplomacy and downshifting the gearshift lever of rhetoric, to remain neutral, but it became increasingly obvious that the nation was going to get into a war, especially since it was almost 1812. A worried nation turned its eyes anxiously toward Thomas Jefferson, then had a good laugh at its own expense when it realized that he was no longer the president. He had been replaced by President James Something, Monroe or Madison, who immediately placed the country on a war footing.[2]

THE WAR OF 1812

The War of 1812 began very badly, with British troops marching right into Washington and setting fire to it, severely disrupting restaurant operations and forcing hundreds of lobbyists to eat in the suburbs. But soon the tide started to turn the Americans' way, thanks in no small part to the ef-

[2]Whatever that means.

forts of the nation's first defense contractor, Ye Olde General Dynamics Corporation, which signed a $23.7 million contract to produce a vital new weapons system, the X-97 laser-controlled "Thunderfire" Musket, an innovative concept that promised to give U.S. soldiers a real technical edge on the field of battle. Unfortunately it was not ready for actual testing until 1957, when it blew up.

THE TREATY OF GHENT

This sounds pretty boring to us so we're just going to skip right over it.

DISCUSSION QUESTIONS

1. Define the following: "dirtbag."
2. Just who *is* Kitty Carlisle, anyway?

FASCINATING HISTORICAL SIDENOTE
TO HISTORY

During the War of 1812, a young poet named Francis "Scott" Key watched the battle for Fort "Mac" Henry, and he was so moved by the sight of the American flag still waving in the dawn's early light that he wrote the immortal words that Americans still proudly sing today:

Take me out to the ball game
Take me out with the croooowwwwd . . .

CHAPTER NINE

Barging Westward

THE FIRST major president to be elected after the War of 1812 was President Monroe Doctrine, who became famous by developing the policy for which he is named. This policy, which is still in effect today, states that:

1. Other nations are *not allowed* to mess around with the internal affairs of nations in this hemisphere.
2. But we are.
3. Ha-ha-ha.

President Doctrine also purchased Florida from Spain for $5 million. Unfortunately, like many first-time buyers of vast New World territories, he failed to inspect the property first; by the time he found out that Florida mostly consisted of swamps infested with armor-piercing mosquitoes the size of Volvo station wagons, Spain had already deposited the check.

In 1816, a political party called the Federalists nominated for president a man named Rufus King, then ceased to exist. The year 1819 saw the occurrence of the aptly named Panic of 1819, which was caused when the growing nation woke up in the middle of the night thinking it had a term paper due. Fortunately this turned out to be just a dream, and things remained fairly calm until 1825, which saw the election of yet another person named John Adams, who was backed by the Party to Elect Only Presidents Named John Adams.

Meanwhile, hardy settlers continued to move westward and discover new virgin lands, unconquered and unclaimed by anybody, unless you counted the Native Americans, which these hardy settlers did not. And, anyhow, before long there were even fewer to count. Soon they had settled a number of territories—Missouri, Indiana, Illinois, Guam—and they were clamoring to become official states so they could start electing legislatures and having state mottoes and official state insects and stuff. But Congress could not readily agree on a procedure for admitting states to the union. The northern politicians felt it should be a simple ceremony, with maybe a small reception afterward; the southerners felt it should be more of a fraternity-style initiation, with new states being forced to do wacky stunts such as get up and sing "She'll Be Comin' Round the Mountain When She Comes" naked. Finally the impasse was broken by means of the Missouri Compromise, under which it was agreed that one half of the people would pronounce it "Missour-EE" and the other half would pronounce it "Missour-UH."

In 1828 Andrew "Stonewall" Jackson was elected president with the support of the Party to Elect Presidents with Stupid Nicknames. His running mate was South Carolinian John C. "Those Little Flies That Sometimes Get in Your Nose" Calhoun, a bitter rival of Secretary of State Martin "Van" Buren, who, with the backing of the brilliant orator Daniel "The Brilliant Orator" Webster, was able to persuade Jackson to replace Calhoun with Van Buren on the 1832 ticket, little aware that Denise and her periodontist were secretly meeting at the same motel where Rhonda had revealed to Dirk that she was in fact the sex-changed former Green Beret who fathered the half-Vietnamese twins that Lisa left in the O'Hare baggage-claim area the night she left to get her Haitian divorce and wound up as a zombie instead, thus resulting in the formation by Henry Clay of the Whig party. Their slogan was "Tippecanoe and Tyler, Too," and they meant every word of it.

None of this would have been possible, of course, without the continued contributions of women and minority groups.

THE FEDERAL BANKING CRISIS OF 1837

Trust us: This was even more boring than the Treaty of Ghent.

CULTURE

Meanwhile, culture was continuing to occur in some areas. In New England, for example, essayist Henry David Thoreau created an enduring masterpiece of American philosophical thought when, rejecting the stifling influences of civilization, he went off to live all alone on Walden Pond, where, after two years of an ascetic and highly introspective life, he was eaten by turtles. That did not stop the march of culture. Authors such as James Fenimore Cooper (*Pippi Leatherstocking, Hiawatha, Natty Bumppo Gets Drunk and Shoots His Own Leg*), Henry Wadsworth Longfellow (*Ludicrously Repetitious Poems That Nobody Ever Finishes*), and Herman Melville (*Moby-Dick, Moby-Dick II, Moby-Dick vs. the Atomic Bat from Hell*) cranked out a series of literary masterpieces that will be remembered as long as they are required reading in high school English classes.

Tremendous advances were also being made in technology. A nautical inventor named Robert Fulton came up with the idea of putting a steam engine on a riverboat. Naturally it sank like a stone, thus creating one of many underwater hazards that paved the way for a young man named Samuel Clemens, who got a job standing on the front of riverboats, peering into the water, and shouting out literary pseudonyms such as "George Eliot!" The steam engine also played a vital role in the development of the famous "Iron Horse," which could haul heavy loads, but which also tended to produce the famous "Monster Piles of Iron Droppings" and thus was eventually replaced by the locomotive.

Tremendous strides were also being taken in the area of communication. With the invention of the rotary press, newspapers were made available not just to the wealthy literate elite, but also to the average low-life scum, who were suddenly able to keep abreast, through pioneering populist papers like the *New York Post,* of such national issues as NAB PAIR IN NUN STAB and LINK PORN SLAY TO EYE SLICE MOB. Another major advance in communication was the telegraph, which was invented by Samuel Morse, who also devised the code that is named after him: "pig Latin." Wires were soon being strung across the vast continent, and by October 8 a message could be transmitted from New York to California, carried by courageous Pony Express riders, who galloped full speed on courageous horses that would often get as far as thirty feet before they would fall off the wires and splat courageously onto the ground.

This created a growing awareness of the practical value of roads, and in 1809 work began on the nation's first highway, the Long Island Expressway, which is scheduled for completion next year.[1] In 1825, New York completed the Erie Canal, which connected Buffalo and Albany, thus enabling these two exciting cities to trade bargeloads of slush. The Erie Canal was an instant financial success, and became even more profitable fourteen years later, when a sharp young engineer suggested filling it with water.

"MANIFEST DESTINY"

"Manifest destiny" is a phrase you see in a lot of history books. Another one is "Fifty-four-forty or fight."

THE FORMATION OF TEXAS

At this point Mexico owned the territory that we now call "Texas," which consisted primarily of what we now call "dirt." Gradually, however, it began to fill up with Americans, who developed a unique frontier life-style based on drinking Pearl beer, going "wooo-EEEE!" real loud, and making cash payments to football players. This irritated the Mexican government, which sent a general named Santa Anna (SAN-ta ANN-a) up to attack the Texans at the Alamo (AL-a-mo), where, in one of the most heroic (he-RO-ic) scenes in American

---

[1] Barring unforeseen delays.

history, the legendary Davy Crockett (played by Fess Parker) used his legendary rifle, "Betsy" (played by "Denise"), as a club in a futile (STUpid) effort to fend off Santa Anna's troops. But the tragedy served as a blessing in disguise, because a short time later the legendary Sam Houston, showing that he had learned the harsh lesson of the Alamo, ordered his troops to try using their rifles as *rifles*. Not only did they rout the Mexicans, but they went on to defeat Oklahoma in the Cotton Bowl. And thus Texas was born, although it was not permitted to enter the union for ten more years, because of NCAA violations.

At this point the president of the United States, a stud named James K. Polk, declared war against Mexico. Don't ask us why. We are a history book, not a mind reader. This resulted in the Treaty of Guadalupe Hidalgo (GUA-da . . . oh, NE-ver MIND), under which the United States got the rest of the Southwest and California, and Mexico got smaller.

THE RUSH TO CALIFORNIA

One day in the winter of 1848, a worker was digging in a pond on the northern California farm of Swiss immigrant Johann Sutter. Suddenly the man stopped and stared, for there, gleaming through the muck on his shovel blade, was a discovery that was to transform the entire California territory almost overnight: a movie camera. Word of the discovery spread like wildfire, and soon thousands of actors, agents, producers, and so forth were rushing westward, overburdening the territory's limited restaurant facilities and causing the price of valet parking to skyrocket. Soon there were more than a hundred thousand residents, which raised the issue: Should California be declared a state? Or, in this case, maybe even a separate planet?

These were just some of the storm clouds now gathering over the nation's political landscape. For meanwhile, back east, the cold front of moral outrage was moving inexorably toward the low-pressure system of southern economic interests, creating another of those frontal systems of conflict that would inevitably result in a violent afternoon or evening thundershower of carnage. Also, it was time for the Civil War.

DISCUSSION QUESTIONS

1. In the song "She'll Be Comin' Round the Mountain When She Comes," why do they announce so cheerfully that they intend to "kill the old red rooster when she comes"? Is it some kind of ritual thing? Or is it that they just hate the old red rooster, because maybe it pecked them or something when they were children, and now they're just using the fact that she's comin' round the mountain as an excuse to kill it?
2. An-cay oo-yay eak-spay ig-pay atin-lay? Explain.
3. Define the following: "Wooo-EEEE!"

CHAPTER TEN

The Civil War: A Nation Pokes Itself in the Eyeball

THE SEEDS of the Civil War were sown in the late eighteenth century when Eli Whitney invented the "cotton gin," a machine capable of turning cotton into gin many times faster than it could be done by hand. This created a great demand for cotton-field workers, whom the South originally attempted to recruit by placing "help wanted" advertisements in the newspaper:

ATTENTION SELF-STARTERS!

Are you that special "can-do" kind of guy or gal who's looking for a chance to work extremely hard under horrible conditions for your entire life without getting paid and being severely beaten whenever we feel like it, plus we get to keep your children? To find out more about this exciting career opportunity, contact: The South.

Oddly enough, this advertisement failed to produce any applicants, and so the South decided to go with slavery. Many people argued that slavery was inhuman and cruel and should be abolished, but the slave owners argued that it wasn't so bad, and that in fact the slaves actually were *happy,* the evidence for this being that they sometimes rattled their chains in a rhythmic fashion.

By the mid-nineteenth century, slavery was the topic of heated debate among just about everybody in the country except of course the actual slaves, most of whom were busy either working or fleeing through swamps. The crisis deepened in 1850, when President Zachary Taylor died of cholera, fueling fears that we forgot to mention his election in the previous chapter. Taylor's death led to the presidency of a man whose name has since become synonymous, in American history, with the term "Millard Fillmore": Millard Fillmore.

HIGHLIGHTS OF
THE FILLMORE ADMINISTRATION
1. The Earth did not crash into the Sun.

After Fillmore came Franklin Pierce and James Buchanan, who as far as we can tell were both president at the same time. This time-saving measure paved the way for the election of Abraham Lincoln, who was popular with the voters because he possessed an extremely rustic set of origins.

THE ORIGINS OF ABRAHAM LINCOLN

Lincoln's family was poor. He was born in a log cabin. And when we say "a log cabin," we are talking about a cabin that consisted entirely of *one single log.* That is how poor Lincoln's family was. When it rained, everybody had to lie down under the log, the result being that Lincoln grew up to be very long and narrow, which turned out to be the ideal physique for splitting rails. Young Abe would get out there with his ax, and he'd split hundreds of rails at a time, and people would come from miles around. "Dammit, Lincoln," they'd say, "those rails cost good money!" But in the end they forgave young Abe, because he had the ax.

He was also known for his honesty. In one famous historical anecdote, Lincoln was tending store, and a customer accidentally left his change on the counter, and young Abe picked it up and walked fourteen miles with it, only to glance down and realize that his face was on the penny. This anecdote gave Lincoln the nickname that was to serve him so well in politics—"Old Ironsides"— and it earned him an invitation to appear as a contestant on *The Lincoln-Douglas Debates,* the most popular show of the era. Lincoln was able to get to the bonus round, where he correctly answered the question "How much is four score plus seven?," thus winning the Samsonite luggage *and* the presidency of the United States.

This resulted in yet another famous historical anecdote. When Lincoln assumed the presidency, he was clean-shaven, but one day he got a letter from a little girl suggesting that he grow a beard. So he did, and he thought it looked pretty good, so he decided to keep it. A short while later, he got another letter from the little girl, this time suggesting that he wear mascara and rouge and maybe a simple string of pearls. Fortunately, just then the Civil War broke out.

THE CIVIL WAR

This was pretty depressing. Brother fought against brother, unless he had no male siblings, in which case he fought against his sister. Sometimes he would even take a shot at his cousin. Sooner or later, this resulted in a horrendous amount of devastation, particularly in the South, where things got so bad that Clark Gable, in what is probably the most famous scene from the entire Civil War, turned to Vivien Leigh, and said: "Frankly, my dear, I don't think we're in Kansas anymore." This epitomized the feeling of despair that was widespread in the Confederacy as the war ended, and it left a vast reservoir of bitterness toward the North. But as the old saying goes, "Time heals all wounds," and in the more than 120 years that have passed since the Civil War ended, most of this bitterness gradually gave way to subdued loathing, which is where we stand today.

RECONSTRUCTION

After the Civil War came Reconstruction, a period during which the South was transformed, through a series of congressional acts, from a totally segregated region where blacks had no rights into a totally segregated region where blacks were supposed to have rights but did not. Much of this progress occurred during the administration of President Ulysses S. Grant, who in 1868 defeated a person named Horatio Seymour in a race where both candidates had the backing of the Let's Elect Presidents with Comical First Names party, whose members practically wet their pants with joy in 1876 over the election of Rutherford B. Hayes, who went on to die—you can look this up—in a place called Fremont, Ohio. Clearly the troubled nation had nowhere to go except up.

DISCUSSION QUESTIONS

1. If he had a beard, where would he apply the rouge?

FUN CLASSROOM PROJECT

See if you can name the causes of the Civil War.

Answer: "Earl" and "Dexter."

CHAPTER ELEVEN

The Nation Enters Chapter Eleven

THE END OF the Civil War paved the way for what Mark Twain, with his remarkable knack for coining the perfect descriptive phrase, called "the post–Civil War era." This was a period unlike any that had preceded it. For one thing, it occurred later on. Also it was an Age of Invention. Perhaps the most important invention was the brainchild of Thomas "Alva" Edison, a brilliant New Jerseyan who, in 1879, astounded the world when he ran an electrical current through a carbonized cotton filament inside a glass globe, thus creating the first compact-disc player. Unfortunately it broke almost immediately and did not come back from the repair shop for nearly a century.[1] But this did not stop the prolific Edison from numerous other electronic breakthroughs that we now take for granted, including: the Rate Increase; the Limited Warranty; the Eight "C" Batteries That Are Not Included; the Instructions That Are Badly Translated from Japanese; and the Newspaper Ad Featuring Four Thousand Tiny Blurred Pictures of What Appears to Be the Same VCR. For these achievements, Edison was awarded, after his death, one of the highest honors that can be bestowed upon a dead American citizen: A service plaza off the New Jersey Turnpike was named after him. Parts of it still stand today.[2]

Another famous genius of the era was Alexander Graham Bell System, who in some specific year beginning with "18" invented the area code, thus paving the way for long distance, without which modern telephone-company commercials would not be possible. Originally there was only one area code, called "1" (see map on next page), but over the years new ones were added steadily, and telephone-company researchers now foresee the day when, thanks to modern computers, every telephone in the nation will be a long-distance call from every other telephone, even if it's in the same house.

[1] And it still didn't work right.
[2] The first is named for Marvin Kitman, the second for Al Capone.

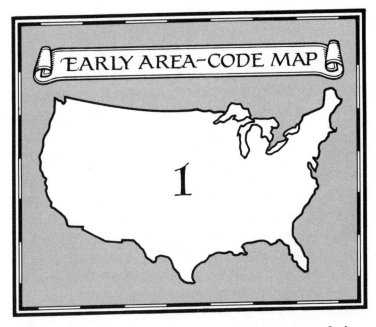

Meanwhile, the nation's rural areas were being greatly affected by the McCormick reaper, which was invented by Cyrus McCormick and paved the way for the Midwest, a group of flat Protestant states containing an enormous amount of agriculture in the form of wheat. Formerly, to reap a single acre of wheat, a farmer would have to work for four days, with the help of two farmhands driving six mules. But now he could sit back and relax as the reaper roared through as many as ten acres per hour, reaping the living hell out of everything that stood in its path, occasionally spitting out bits of mule fur or farmhand clothing, which could easily be reassembled thanks to the sewing machine, invented by Elias Howe. "Don't

ask me Howe it works!'' he used to say, over and
over, until finally somebody, we think his wife,
shot him in the head with a revolver, invented by
Samuel Colt.

McCormick's invention was so successful that
by the early 1870s the Midwest was *disappearing*
under an enormous mound of reaped wheat, and it
became clear that some kind of efficient method
was needed to get it to the big cities, where it
could be converted into sandwiches, which had
been invented earlier in England by Samuel
Bacon, Lettuce, and Tomato. This caused Congress to authorize work on the first transcontinen-
tal railroad corporation, Amtrak. Two work
crews began laying rails, one starting on the East
Coast and the other on the West Coast. It was
hard going. The crews endured broiling heat and
bitter cold, often simultaneously. But they persevered, and finally, on October 8, the two crews met
at Promontory Point, Utah, where, in a moving
and historic ceremony, top railroad executives
gathered to explain to them that they were supposed to be nailing the rails *down,* for God's sake.

But even this setback did not prevent women
and minority groups from achieving many notable
achievements.

THE RISE OF HEAVY INDUSTRY

Around this time heavy industry started to rise,
thanks to the work of heavy industrialists such as

Andrew "Dale" Carnegie, who made a fortune
going around the country holding seminars in
which he taught people how to win friends by
making steel. Another one was John D. Rockefel-
ler, who invented oil and eventually created a mo-
nopoly, culminating in 1884 when he was able to
put hotels on both Park Place *and* Boardwalk.
This made him so rich that everybody started hating him, and he was ultimately forced to change
his name to "Exxon."

As heavy industrialism became more popular,
large horrible factories were built in eastern cities. The workers—often minority women and children—toiled under grueling, dangerous conditions
for twelve hours a day, seven days a week, for an
average weekly salary of only $1.80, out of which
they had to "voluntarily" give 85 cents to the
United Fund. On top of this, the factory workers
were subjected to one of the most cruel and inhumane labor concepts ever conceived of by the mind
of industrial man: vending-machine food. The
suffering this caused can only be imagined by us
fortunate modern corporation employees, but we
can get some idea of what it was like by reading
this chilling excerpt from a nineteenth-century
New York factory worker's diary:

> Nobody knows where the food comes from, or even
> if it really is food. There is a machine that dis-
> penses liquids that are allegedly "coffee," "tea,"
> "hot chocolate," and even "soup," which all come

from the same orifice and *all taste exactly the same.*
Another machine dispenses bags containing a
grand total of maybe three potato chips each, and
packages of crackers smeared with a bizarre substance called "cheez," which is the same bright-
orange color as marine rescue equipment. The
machine for some reason is constructed in such a
way that it drops these items from a great height,
causing the contents, already brittle with age, to
shatter into thousands of pieces. Also half the
time it just eats your money, and *forget* about getting a refund. . . .

Conditions such as these resulted in the Labor
Movement, the most important leader of which
was Samuel Gompers. And even if he wasn't the
most important, he definitely had the best name.
We could just say it over and over: Gompers
Gompers Gompers. This would be an excellent
name for a large dog.[3] "Gompers!" we can just
hear ourselves yelling. "You put that Federal Express man down *right now*!" Nevertheless it was to
be a long, hard struggle before the Labor Movement was to win even minimal concessions from
the big industrialists—years of strikes and violence and singing traditional Labor Movement
protest songs such as "Take This Job and Shove
It." But it was the courage of these early labor
pioneers that ultimately made possible the working conditions and wages and benefits that Ameri-

[3]Such as a Labrador retriever.

can factory workers would probably be enjoying today if the industrialists hadn't moved their manufacturing operations to Asia.

THE SETTLEMENT OF THE WEST

When the Civil War ended, the West was still a region of great wildness, a fact that had earned it the nickname "The Great Plains." In this rough, untamed environment had emerged the cowboy, a hard-ridin' straight-shootin' rip-snortin' cow-punchin' breed of hombre who was to become the stuff of several major cigarette promotions. To this day you can walk up to any schoolboy and mention one of those legendary Old West names—Wyatt Earp, "Wild Bill" Hickok, Gary Cooper, "Quick Draw" McGraw, Luke Skywalker—and chances are the schoolboy, as he has been taught to do, will scream for help, and you will be arrested on suspicion of being a pervert. So maybe you better just take our word for it.

Nevertheless, the West was gradually being settled. The federal government had acquired assorted western territories like Utah through treaties with the Native American inhabitants under which the United States got the land and the Native Americans got a full thirty minutes' head start before the army came after them. In 1889 the U.S. government opened up the Oklahoma territory, which resulted in the famous

"Oklahoma land rush" as thousands of would-be settlers came racing in to look around, resulting in the famous "rush to get the hell back out of Oklahoma."

Another important acquisition was made in 1867, when Secretary of State Seward Folly purchased Alaska for $7 million, which at the time seemed like a lot of money but which today we recognize as being about one third the cost of a hotel breakfast in Anchorage. Alaska was originally a large place located way the hell up past Canada, but this proved to be highly inconvenient for mapmakers, who in 1873 voted to make it smaller and put it in a little box next to Hawaii right off the coast of California, which is where it is today (see map on next page).

While all this expansion was going on, presidents were continuing to be elected right on schedule in 1868, 1872, 1876, and so on, and we're pretty sure that at least one of them was named Rutherford. Also during this era the large eastern cities began to experiment with a new form of government, favored by newspaper cartoonists, called the Easily Caricatured Corrupt Spherical Bosses Weighing a Minimum of 400 Pounds system. This system was very unpopular, because it resulted in an unresponsive government filled with overpaid drones and hacks who, no matter how little they did or how badly they did it, could be removed from their jobs only by the unelected bosses. The result of this discontent, the Reform

Movement, produced the modern "Civil Service" system, under which drones and hacks can be removed only by nuclear weapons.

In 1880 the voters elected a president named Chester, and in 1884 they elected one named Grover. We now think this might have been caused by a comet. Also there was a hideous hassle involving William Jennings Bryan and something called the "gold standard," but every time anybody tries to explain it to us we get a terrible headache. We have the same problem with the concept of "second cousins."

DISCUSSION QUESTIONS

1. Can you name another famous person for whom a service plaza is named? *(Hint: Vince Lombardi.)*
2. What is "rip-snortin'," anyway? Do you think it should be legal?
3. Do you have any second cousins? So what?

CHAPTER TWELVE

Groping
Toward Empire

B Y 1890 THE WEST had been tamed and could even obey simple commands such as "Sit!" Now the United States was no longer an infant nation, but a mighty young colossus, bestriding[1] the continent—in the words of Mark Twain—"like some kind of mighty young colossus or something." America was the Land of Opportunity, and its symbol was the Statue of Liberty, a gift from the French that had been dedicated in 1886 in a spectacular ceremony featuring a thousand John Philip Sousa impersonators. The statue was placed in New York Harbor, where its raised torch served as a welcoming beacon of hope and

[1]Unless there is no such word.

freedom to millions of oppressed and downtrodden
fish. Then somebody came up with the idea of taking it out of the water and putting it on an island,
and from that day on it was a major tourist at-
traction for European immigrants, who flocked to
America by the millions, drawn by the promise expressed in the stirring poem by Emma Lazarus:

> Give me your low-income individuals
> Tired of these dense tempest-tost huddles
> Yearning to get the hell off the boat
> And retch all over the teeming shore

And so they came—the Irish, the Italians, the
Jews, the Germans, the Greeks, the Klingons, the
Marcoses—lured by tales of good jobs and streets
paved with gold and plenty of closet space. But
what they found was quite different. What they
found was New York City—a frantic, bustling
place; a giant (to use Mark Twain's phrase) "fondue pot" in which people from many nationalities,
crowded together by necessity, gradually began to
realize that despite their differences in language,
custom, and religion, they all, in the end, hated
each other. Also the Americans who already lived
here, except for Emma Lazarus, were not exactly
crazy about immigrants either. And so the new
citizens formed neighborhoods, and they moved
into cramped tenement apartments, and a lot of
them still live there. They don't move out even

when they die, because New York apartments are too valuable to give up.

As New York City grew and prospered, it began to form corporations, enormous "super-companies" whose vast resources enabled them to do something that smaller firms could only dream of: transfer people. This created a demand for new cities, which soon flourished in places such as Minneapolis, Chicago, and even, for a brief period, Cleveland.

But perhaps the most important new industrial area was Detroit, founded by Henry Ford I, who also invented the Ford, forerunner to today's Isuzu. The key to Ford's success as an industrialist was his discovery of the assembly line, which worked on a simple principle: Instead of having the workers move from place to place to assemble the cars, he had the *cars* move from place to place to assemble the *workers.* For some reason this proved to be extremely efficient, and in 1913 the Ford Motor Company began cranking out thousands of the famous "Model T." By modern automotive standards, the Model T was very primitive: It had no electric starter, no radio, no heater, no air conditioner, no brakes, no transmission, no engine, and no wheels. The only way to get it to actually move was to have four or five burly men pick it up and stagger down the street. But it was affordable, and people bought it like crazy. "What the hell," they said. "There's nowhere to go anyway, here in 1913."

Meanwhile, another historic transportation development was taking place in Kitty Hawk, North Carolina, a desolate spit of sand where two young bicycle mechanics named Wilbur and Orville Wright Brothers had gone to escape from people who teased them about their first names. Also they were interested in heavier-than-air flight. They used to sit on the dunes for hours, studying the soaring sea gulls, hoping to learn the aerodynamic secret that kept them aloft. And then one historic day, a shout rang out: "I've got it, Wilbur! They're using propellers driven by gasoline engines!" And then another shout: "I'm not Wilbur! *You're* Wilbur!" This was after many days on the dunes.

Nevertheless they went ahead and built their "flying machine," and on October 8, they were ready for their first flight. Unfortunately, it had to be canceled because of equipment problems at O'Hare, but they persevered, and finally came the historic moment when Wilbur, or possibly Orville, managed to get the frail, odd-looking craft airborne as far as Atlanta, where he changed to a connecting flight,[2] thus successfully launching the Aviation Age, although his luggage was never found.

This new spirit of soaring optimism could also be detected in the arts, most notably in the work of Horatio Alger, who wrote a series of very popu-

[2]Daily except Sunday; featuring "snack" service.

lar "rags to riches" stories in which a poor but intelligent young man is able, through hard work and honesty, to locate the Wizard of Oz. A number of talented American painters whose names escape us at the moment sprang up and created a number of important paintings that we probably still cherish today. The same thing happened with sculpture, not to mention women and minority groups, who continued to make gigantic contributions despite continuing to have no more legal rights than gravel. All in all, the turn of the century was an exciting, boisterous time for America, a raucous cacophony of energy and invention, idealism and hucksterism—in short, to repeat the words of the brilliant poet and chocolate manufacturer Walt Whitman, it was "loud." This caused imperialism to wake up.

THE AWAKENING OF IMPERIALISM

The first thing American imperialism noticed when it woke up was Cuba. At the time Cuba technically belonged to Spain, which alert readers will remember as the country that, in previous confrontations with the United States, had proved to be about as effective, militarily, as a tuna casserole. So it seemed like the ideal time to barge down there and free Cuba from the yoke of Spanish imperialism by placing it under the yoke of U.S. imperialism, the only problem being that at the time the United States did not have what international lawyers refer to, in technical legalistic terms, as a "reason." So things looked very bleak indeed until one day in 1898 when, in a surprise stroke of good fortune, the U.S. battleship *Maine* exploded and sank in Havana harbor.

Immediately the American news media, showing a dedication to accuracy and objectivity that would not be surpassed until nearly a century later (when the *Weekly World News,* available at supermarkets everywhere, reported that a Turkish farmer and four of his cows had been eaten by a giant purple flower from space), announced that the *Maine* had definitely, no question about it, been sunk by Spain. Soon the rallying cry went up from coast to coast: "Give 'em hell, Harry!" This inspired William McKinley, who had been elected president of the United States earlier in this chapter while we were not paying attention, to issue an ultimatum[3] to Spain in which he demanded a number of concessions.

Spain immediately agreed to all the demands, an act of treachery that the United States clearly could not tolerate. It was time to declare:

THE SPANISH-AMERICAN WAR

Although the Spanish-American War was over in less time than it takes to order Oriental food for

---

[3]From the Latin, meaning "a kind of a thing that a person issues."

six people by telephone, it ranks with the successful invasion of Grenada as one of the country's
mightiest military accomplishments. The highlight
came when Teddy "Theodore" Roosevelt led his
band of rough-riding cavalry persons, nicknamed
the "Boston Celtics," in the famous Charge up
San Juan Hill, which turned out to be unoc-
cupied, thus paving the way for the famous
Charge Down the Other Side of San Juan Hill.
After suffering several such military setbacks,
Spain surrendered and gave the United States
control of not only Cuba, but also Puerto Rico,
the Philippines, Guam, Wake Island, Australia,
Snooze Island, Antarctica, France, and the Crab
Nebula. "Go ahead, take everything," said Spain.
"We're going to get drunk and become a third-
rate power."

But not the United States. Having flexed the
triceps of its newfound military might and, aided
by the steroidal substance of nationalistic senti-
ment, successfully bench-pressed the five-hun-
dred-pound weight of international expansionism,
the United States was now eager to play a dominant role on the international stage, with an option for the film rights. What the nation needed,
as it entered this new era, was a dynamic leader
capable of commanding this globe-begirdling[4]
young empire, but who?[5] That was the question

[4]Or whatever.
[5]Or possibly "whom?"

everybody was standing around asking him- or herself in 1901 when, in another amazing stroke of good luck, an anarchist shot William McKinley, who revealed, on his deathbed, that he had been elected president in 1900, and that his vice president was a man who happened to be not only a war hero, but a descendant of a distinguished family, a public servant, a statesman, a big-game hunter, a naturalist, a husband, a father, a heck of a fine human being, and one of my closest personal friends, I really love this guy, let's give a big Las Vegas welcome to (drum roll) . . .

THEODORE ROOSEVELT

Roosevelt was a Man of Action, not words. The public loved the way he took on the businessmen who ran the big monopolies, or "trusts." Roosevelt would invite these men to the White House and speak very softly, forcing them to lean forward, straining to hear, whereupon Roosevelt would hammer them over the heads with a big stick[6] that he always carried. This was just one of his famous mannerisms, another one being that he often referred to the presidency as a "bully pulpit." Nobody knew what on earth he meant by this, but nobody asked him, either, because of the stick.

Of all Roosevelt's achievements, however, the

[6]Nicknamed "Betsy."

most significant, as measured by total gallonage, was:

THE PANAMA CANAL

In those days, there was no easy way for ships to get from the Atlantic to the Pacific. The usual procedure was for a ship to start picking up a head of steam as it went past Cuba, so it would be going full speed when it rammed into the Isthmus of Panama, sometimes getting eight or even ten feet into the jungle before shuddering to a halt. Clearly the United States needed to build a canal. The problem was that Panama technically belonged to Colombia, which refused to sign a treaty leasing it to the United States. So Roosevelt sent a gunboat filled with marines down to Panama, just on the off chance that a revolution might suddenly break out, and darned if one didn't, two days later. Not only that, but the leaders of the new nation of Panama—talk about lucky breaks!—were absolutely thrilled to have the United States build a canal there. "Really, it's our pleasure," they told the marines, adding, "Don't shoot."

Over the next few years, the marines, in their role as Heavily Armed Ambassadors of Friendship and Fun, were to meet with similar outpourings of cheerful cooperation in Nicaragua, Mexico, the Dominican Republic, Haiti, and other Latin American countries that the United States decided to befriend as complete diplomatic equals in a spirit of mutual respect and without regard for the fact that we could squash them like dung beetles under a cement truck. We were a Happy Hemisphere indeed. It was time to think about branching out.

DISCUSSION QUESTIONS

1. You know what really ticks us off? The way the Boston Celtics bitch and moan whenever a foul is called against them.
2. What does "all in all" mean, anyway?
3. How about: "by and large"?

CHAPTER THIRTEEN

Deep
International
Doo-doo

THE YEAR 1908 saw the election of the first U.S. president to successfully weigh more than three hundred pounds, William Howard Taft, who ran on a platform of reinforced concrete and who, in a stirring inauguration speech, called for "a bacon cheeseburger and a side order of fries." Another important occurrence in the Taft administration was the famous Ballinger-Pinchot Affair, which is truly one of the most fascinating and bizarre episodes in the nation's history, although it is quite frankly none of your business.[1]

After that not much happened until approxi-

---

[1]Especially the part about the dwarf goat.

mately 1912, when Teddy Roosevelt, who had gone
over to Africa to unwind from the pressures of
the presidency by attempting to kill every animal
on the entire continent larger than a wristwatch,
decided he wanted to be president again. So he
came barging back and formed a new party, which
was called the Bull Moose party so as to evoke the
inspirational image of an enormous animal eating
ferns and pooping all over the landscape. Despite
this concept, Teddy lost, which is a real tragedy
because a Bull Moose victory might have started a
whole new trend of giving comical animal names
to political parties, and today we might be seeing
election battles between the Small Hairless Nocturnal Rodent party and the Stench-Emitting
Ox party, and this country would be a *lot* more
fun.

The winner in the 1912 election was Woodrow
Wilson, known to his close friends as "Woodrow
Wilson," who garnered many votes with the popular slogan "Wilson: He'll Eventually Get Us into
World War I." The appeal of this concept was so
strong that Wilson was easily swept into office despite widespread allegations of vote-garnering.

THE SUFFRAGETTE MOVEMENT

Meanwhile, out on the streets, there was a lot of
movement by "suffragettes," a term meaning "girl
suffrages." The suffragettes, led by Susan B. An-

thony Dollar, believed that women should be given the right to vote on the grounds that they could not possibly screw things up worse than men already had. They ultimately achieved their goal by marching around in public wearing hats the size of elementary schools, a tactic later adopted, for reasons that are still unclear, by Queen Elizabeth.

Another major social development of the time was the Temperance Movement, led by Carrie Nation, who headed an organization called Scary-Looking Women with Hatchets. They would swoop down upon saloons and smash all the whiskey bottles, then go back to their headquarters, fire up reefers as big as Roman candles, and laugh until dawn. This resulted in so much social turmoil that in 1918 Congress decided to have a total prohibition on alcohol, which was approved early on a Saturday morning by a vote of 9–2, with 416 members unable to attend because of severe headaches. Thus began the nation's "Noble Experiment," which was eventually judged to be a noble failure and replaced by the current sensible and coherent alcohol policy of showing public-service TV announcements wherein professional sports figures urge people not to drink, interspersed with TV commercials wherein professional sports figures urge people to drink.

But all of this paled by comparison with international tension, which was—get ready for a bulletin here—mounting.

THE CAUSES OF
INTERNATIONAL TENSION

The major cause of international tension was
Europe, which in those days was made up of the
Five (or possibly Six) Major Powers: Great Britain, France, Russia, Germany, the Ottomans, the
Barca-Loungers, and the Austro-Hungarian Empire, an alliance between Australia and Hungary
that was not really all that major a power but was
allowed to participate in international tension
anyway because it had some pretty good restau-
rants. These powers had spent roughly the past
thousand years trying to see who could set the
land speed record for breaking treaties with each
other, and they had been involved in so many complex alliances and double crosses that in 1903, in
one of the more hilarious moments in international diplomacy, France accidentally declared
war on itself.[2] By 1914 Europe was, in the words
of the bad writer Elrod Stooble, "a tinderbox with
a hair trigger just waiting for the other foot to
drop."

And thus the entire continent was extremely
tense and irritable, just generally in a bad mood,
that fateful summer day, October 8, when a young
archduke named Franz Ferdinand chanced to pass
by the fateful spot where a young anarchist
named Gavrilo Princip happened to be standing in
a fateful manner, and, through an unfortunate

[2]And lost.

quirk of fate, got into an argument over who had the silliest name. Not surprisingly, this caused Austro-Hungary to declare war on Serbia, only to be ridiculed by France, Great Britain, and Russia when it was discovered that there actually was no such place as "Serbia." This discovery, needless to say, caused Germany to invade Belgium (one key lesson of history is that virtually *anything,* including afternoon or evening thundershowers, causes Germany to invade Belgium). Soon all of Europe was at war.

In America, the prevailing mood was that this was a truly dumb war and we should stay the hell out of it. Just about everybody agreed on this: the public, the press, barnyard animals, even leading political figures. Anybody who even talked about the *possibility* of the United States getting into this war was considered to be a cretin. In the presidential election campaign of 1916,[3] both President Woodrow Wilson and the Republican nominee, Charles Evans Hughes, went around stating in loud, emotion-choked voices that they were definitely by God not going to get the country into the war. So it was clear that the United States had no choice but to get into the war, which, in 1917, it did. And a darned good thing, too, because the official title of the war turned out to be:

[3]Often referred to by historians as "The Election Where Both Candidates' Names Could Be Read in Either Direction."

"The War to End All Wars"

President Wilson's theory at the time was that
America would march over there and help France
and Britain win the war, and then the winners
would be extremely fair and decent and not take
enormous sums of money or huge chunks of land
from the losers, plus the entire system of world
government would be reformed so that everybody
would live in Peace and Freedom Forevermore.
Needless to say, France and Britain thought this
was the funniest theory they had ever heard, and
they would beg Wilson to tell it again and again
at dinner parties. "Hey Woody!" they'd shriek,
tears of laughter falling into their cognac (CONE-
yak). "Tell us the part where we don't take money
or land!"

The Actual War Itself

The actual war itself was extremely depressing
and in many cases fatal, so we're going follow
Standard History Textbook Procedure for talking
about wars, under which we pretty much skip
over the part where people get killed and instead
make a big deal over what date the treaty was
signed.

The Treaty of Versailles

The Treaty of Versailles (Pa-REE) was signed on
a specific date—our guess would be October
8—and it incorporated Wilson's basic proposals,

except that instead of *not* taking enormous sums of money and huge chunks of land from the losers, the winners at the last minute decided that it would be a better idea if they *did* take enormous sums of money and chunks of land from the losers. Other than that the war accomplished all of America's major objectives, and by 1919 Europe had been transformed, at a cost of only several million dead persons, from a group of nations that hated each other into a group of nations that *really* hated each other. Thus it came as no surprise when, in 1920, American voters overwhelmingly voted to elect a president named Warren G. Harding,[4] who called for a return to "normalcy," which as far as we know is not even a real word.

THE LEAGUE OF NATIONS
Standings as of 1920

COUNTRY	WINS	LOSSES
Austria	0	1
England	1	0
France	1	0
Germany	0	1
United States*	—	—
Serbia**	—	—

*Did not, technically, participate in the League.
**Did not, technically, exist.

[4]Also known as G. Harding Warren.

THE RUSSIAN REVOLUTION

Somewhere along in here the Russians overthrew
the corrupt murdering scumball ruling aristocrats
who for centuries had lived like kings while brutally oppressing the masses, and replaced them
with the communists, who did the same thing but
at least had the decency to wear ill-fitting suits.
Ultimately, of course, this event was to have a
major impact on the United States, but for right
now, the hell with it.

DISCUSSION QUESTIONS

1. A *dwarf* goat?

CHAPTER FOURTEEN

A Nation Gets Funky

THE ERA immediately after World War I came to be known as the "Roaring Twenties," and with good reason: Each of the years had a "twenty" in it, as in 1923, 1925, and so forth. Also there was a lot of wild and zany activity, with "flappers" going to "speakeasies" where they would listen to "jazz," dance the "Charleston," and drink "bathtub gin" until they "puked" all over the "floor." It was a very exciting time, but it also made for an exhausting life-style, which is why you will notice that any people who happened to live through it tend to look kind of elderly.

But all was not fun and games during the twenties. There was also Labor Unrest, caused by coal miners emerging from the ground and making radical demands such as: (1) they should get paid; or, at least (2) they should not have the tunnels collapse on them so often. The coal companies generally responded by bringing in skilled labor negotiators to bargain with the miners' heads using clubs. This often resulted in violence, which forced the federal government, in its role as peacekeeper, to have federal troops shoot at the miners with guns. Eventually the miners realized that they were safer down in the collapsing tunnels, and there was a considerable decline in Labor Unrest.

Another significant accomplishment of the federal government during the twenties was the refinement of high-level corruption, which peaked during the administration of President Harding G. Harding with the famous

TEAPOT DOME SCANDAL

The Teapot Dome Scandal involved a plot of federal land in Wyoming that derives its unusual name from the fact that, if viewed from a certain angle, it appears to be shaped like a scandal. The government had placed a large amount of oil under this land for safekeeping, but in 1921 it was stolen. The mystery was solved later that same evening when an alert customs inspector noticed former Secretary of the Interior Albert Fall attempting to board an oceanliner with a suitcase containing 3.256 trillion barrels of petroleum products, which he claimed had been a "gift" from a "friend." At this point President Harding, showing the kind of class that Richard Nixon can only dream about, died.

Harding's successor was Calvin Coolidge, who was popularly known as "Silent Cal" because that was his nickname. The major accomplishment of the Coolidge administration is a group of humorous anecdotes revolving around the fact that Coolidge hardly ever talked. For example, there's the famous story of the time that Coolidge was sitting next to a woman at a White House dinner and the following hilarious exchange took place:

WOMAN: So, Mr. President. How are you?
COOLIDGE:
WOMAN: Is there something wrong?
COOLIDGE:
WOMAN: Why won't you answer me?
COOLIDGE:
WOMAN: What a cretin.

Another popular humorist of the day was Will Rogers, who used to do an act where he'd twirl a lasso and absolutely slay his audiences with such wry observations as: "The only thing I know is what I read in the papers." Ha-ha! Get it? Neither do we. Must have been something he did with the lasso.

But there was more to the twenties than mere hilarity. A great deal of important breakthroughs were being achieved in the field of culture by giants such as F. Scott Fitzgerald and Ernest Hemingway, who, in 1924, after years of experimentation at their laboratory in Menlo Park, New Jersey, successfully tested the modern American novel, which is still in widespread use today. Poets such as T. S. Eliot and e. e. "buster" cummings were producing a new type of "free-form" verse designed to prove that a poem did not have to be long to be boring. Then, too, in Memphis, Tennessee, the first supermarket, a Piggly Wiggly, was opened. On the West Coast, the motion-picture industry was producing "talkies" featuring such stars as Douglas Fairbanks, Edward G. Robinson, the young Joan Collins, and numerous twitching pieces of film lint magnified to the size of boa constrictors. It was also a Golden Age of Sports, with the most famous hero of them all, of course, being the immortal Babe "Herman" Ruth, who provided what is perhaps baseball's finest moment during the seventh game of the 1927 World Series when, with the score tied and two out, he pointed his bat toward the left-field bleachers, and then, on the very next pitch, in a feat that will live forever, he knocked out the immortal Jack Dempsey.

But no achievement symbolized the spirit of the Roaring Twenties more than that of a tall young

American aviator named, simply, Charles A. Lindbergh. Those of us who are fortunate enough to live in this era of modern commercial aviation, where air travel is extremely safe, thanks to advanced safety procedures such as making the airports so congested that airplanes hardly ever take off, can little appreciate the courage it took for Lindbergh to climb into the cramped cockpit of his single-engine plane, the *Heidy-Ho IV,* and take off into the predawn October 8 gloom over Roosevelt Field, Long Island, towing a banner that said, simply, TAN DON'T BURN WITH COPPERTONE.

It was not an easy flight. Because of air turbulence, there was no beverage-cart service, and it turned out that Lindbergh had already seen the movie.[1] Nevertheless he persevered, and thirty-three hours later, on the afternoon of October 8, he arrived at an airfield near Paris, where, to the joy of a watching world, he plowed into a crowd of French persons at over 140 miles per hour. An instant hero, he returned in triumph for a motorcade ride in New York City, where millions welcomed him, in typical "Big Apple" style, by covering the streets with litter, much of which can still be seen today. But little did the cheering crowds realize, as streams of ticker tape fluttered down from office windows, that within just two years, the falling paper would be replaced by fall-

[1] *The Poseidon Adventure.*

ing stockbrokers. If the crowds *had* realized this, of course, they would have stayed to watch.

DISCUSSION QUESTIONS

1. What do coal companies *do* with the coal, anyway? You never see it for sale.
2. Is "Big Apple" a stupid nickname, or what?

CHAPTER FIFTEEN

Severe Economic Bummerhood

THE DAY the stock market crashed—October 8, 1929—will forever be etched on the Etch a Sketch of the American consciousness as "the day the stock market crashed," or sometimes "Black Tuesday." For on that fateful day, the nation's seemingly prosperous economy was revealed to be merely a paper tiger with feet of clay living in a straw house of cards that had cried "wolf" once too often. Although this would not become clear for some time.

Oh, there had been warning signs. Just a few weeks before Black Tuesday, there had been Mauve Wednesday, which was followed, only two days later, by Dark Navy Blue with Thin Diagonal Yellow Stripes Friday. But most Americans

paid little heed[1] to these events, choosing instead
to believe the comforting words of President Herbert Hoover Dam, who, in a reassuring nationwide
radio broadcast, said: "Everybody STAY CALM,
because there is NOTHING TO WORRY
ABOUT! Do you HEAR ME?? *NOTHING!!* HA-
HA-HA-HA-HA-HA-HA [*click*]."

What were the underlying causes of the Crash?
To truly understand the answer to this question,
we must examine:

THE UNDERLYING CAUSES
OF THE CRASH

The stock market of the 1920s was very different
from the stock market of today. Back then, the
market was infested by greed-crazed slimeballs,
get-rich-quick speculators with the ethical standards of tapeworms, who shrieked "buy" and
"sell" orders into the telephone with no concern
whatsoever for the nation's long-term financial
well-being. Whereas today they use computers.

Another big flaw in the stock market of 1929
was the practice of "buying on margin." To illus-
trate how this worked, let's take a hypothetical example. Let's say Investor A had x amount of
dollars that he wished to invest in the stock market. He would pick up telephone B, dial 123–4567,

---

[1]"Little Heed" would be a good name for a rock band. Also
"Short Shrift."

and tell stockbroker C he wanted to buy stock "on margin" in Company D. And the stockbroker would sell it to him, *even though Company D did not really exist.* We just made it up, for this hypothetical example.[2]

Clearly, this kind of thing could not go on forever, and on Black Tuesday, it did not. As stock prices plummeted, panic selling spread. A number of speculators, realizing that their dreams of wealth had turned to ashes and seeing no hope of repaying their debts, hurled themselves from their office windows. Even this failed to brighten the national mood. Because it was becoming increasingly apparent that the Roaring Twenties were over, and that a new era had arrived: an era of unemployment, poverty, social turmoil, despair, and—worst of all—Shirley Temple movies. And thus began what became known, following a highly successful "Name That Era" contest sponsored by the *New York World Herald Journal Telegram-Bugle and Harmonica,* as:

THE GREAT DEPRESSION

The Great Depression was horrible. Ask the people who lived through it. Or, don't even bother to ask. Just stand next to them for more than two minutes, and they'll tell you about it.

"It was hard, during the Great Depression,"

---

[2]Although as of yesterday it was up two points in active trading.

they'll say. "We had nothing to eat except floor sweepings and we walked eighteen miles to school. Even if the school was only two miles away, we'd have to walk back and forth nine times, because times were bad, and you had no choice, so you worked hard for every nickel, which in those days would buy you two tickets to a movie plus four boxes of popcorn plus a used Buick sedan, but of course we couldn't afford it because Dad only made two dollars and fifty-seven cents per year and our shoes were made out of grapefruit rinds, but we never complained, no, we were happy, because we had *values* in those days, and if you had values you didn't need a lot of money or food or toilet paper, which was a luxury in those days to the point where we'd get through a whole year— this was a family of eleven—on just *six squares* of toilet paper, because we had this system where if you had to . . . HEY! Come back here!"

As the federal government began to recognize the seriousness of the situation, it swung into action with the historic enactment, in 1930, of

THE HAWLEY-SMOOT TARIFF

Quite frankly we have no idea what this is, but we think it has a wonderful ring to it, and we just like to see it in large bold letters:

THE HAWLEY-SMOOT TARIFF

And yet, as the weeks dragged into months and the economy continued to founder, it soon became clear that some economic "medicine" even more potent than

THE HAWLEY-SMOOT TARIFF

would be needed to get the nation "back on its feet." This paved the way for the historic election of 1932. The Republicans, showing the kind of sensitivity they are famous for, renominated President Hoover Dam, who pledged that, if elected, he would flee to the Bahamas. The Democrats countered by nominating Franklin Delano Roosevelt—or, as he was affectionately known, "J.F.K."—who ran under the slogan "Let's Elect Another President Named 'Roosevelt' and Confuse the Hell out of Future Generations of Students." The voters responded overwhelmingly, and Roosevelt was elected in a mammoth landslide that unfortunately left him confined to a wheelchair for the rest of his life.

Nevertheless he began immediately to combat the Depression, implementing a series of bold and sweeping new programs that came to be known, collectively, as:

THE HAWLEY-SMOOT TARIFF

No! Sorry! We can't control ourselves. The programs implemented by Roosevelt were of course called the "New Deal," which consisted of the following:

1. *Bank Protection*—A major problem during the Depression was that people kept trying to get their money out of banks. To put a stop to this kind of thing, the government instituted modern banking regulations, under which:
   * The banks are never open when it might be convenient.
   * The customer is never sure what his bank's name is, since they keep changing it, usually from something like "The First Formal Federal National State Bank of Savings Loans and Of Course Trust" to something like "InterContiBankAmeriTransWestSouthNorthCorp."
   * There are always stupid people in line ahead of you trying to cash checks from the Bank of Yemen and using underwear labels for identification.
2. *Job Creation*—The government instituted a massive program of public works, under which tens of thousands of men and women were put to work strewing barricades and traffic cones on all the major roads in America, then using red flags to give halfhearted and confusing signals to motorists and sometimes waving them directly into the path of oncoming traffic. These projects are still fully operational today.

3. *The Infield Fly Rule*—Under this program, when there is a runner on first or second base and there are fewer than two out, and the batter is the son of the runner's first cousin, then the batter and the runner are legally considered "second cousins."

Not surprisingly, these programs had an immediate impact on the Great Depression. And although some members of Congress charged that Roosevelt was overstepping his legal authority, he was able to win them over by inviting them to the White House for a series of "Fireside Chats" ("Perhaps, Senator, you would understand these policies better if Ernst and Victor moved you even *closer* to the fire?" "NO! PLEASE!").

But even firm measures such as this did not prevent huge clouds of dust kicked up by

THE HAWLEY-SMOOT TARIFF

from covering entire states such as Oklahoma and turning them into a gigantic "Dust Bin," forcing tens of thousands of people to pack up and head toward California, lured by the hope of finding jobs and a new life and maybe some decent sushi. This troubled era was chronicled brilliantly by John Steinbeck in his moving novel *The Grapes of Wrath,* part of a series that also includes *The Pinto Beans of Lust* and *Bloodsucking Death Cabbages from Hell.* And we could go on for days talking about the contributions being made during this period by women and minority groups.

But the bottom line was, things were still not going well. The only really positive aspect of the situation was that at least the nation was at peace. Yet at that very same moment, across the dark, brooding waters of the Atlantic, there was growing concern. "My God, look at those waters!" people were saying. "They're *brooding*!" Clearly this did not bode well for the next chapter, which would see the outbreak of the most terrible and destructive event in the history of Mankind:

THE HAWLEY-SMOOT TARIFF

DISCUSSION QUESTIONS

1. Did you ever see the movie *Attack of the Killer Tomatoes*? Explain.
2. You know how on the evening news they always tell you that the stock market is up in active trading, or off in moderate trading, or trading in mixed activity, or whatever? Well, who gives a shit?

CHAPTER SIXTEEN

Major
Nonhumorous Events
Occur

WHILE THE United States was struggling to get out of the Depression, the nations of Europe were struggling to overcome the horror and devastation and death of World War I so they could go ahead and have World War II. By the 1930s everybody was just about ready, so Germany, showing the kind of spunky "can-do" spirit that has made it so popular over the years, started invading various surrounding nations. Fortunately these were for the most part *small* nations, but Germany's actions nevertheless alarmed Britain and France, which decided to strike back via the bold and clever strategy of signing agreements with Adolf Hitler. Their thinking was: If you can't trust an insane racist paranoid spittle-emitting criminal dictator, whom can you trust?

Shockingly, this strategy did not prove to be effective. In 1939 Germany invaded Poland in retaliation for Poland's flagrant and provocative decision to be right next door. Britain and France then declared war against Germany, which immediately invaded France and managed to conquer it after an epic battle lasting, by some accounts, as long as thirty-five minutes, with the crushing blow coming near the end when Germany's ally, Italy, sent in its much-feared troops, who penetrated nearly two hundred feet into southern France before their truck broke down.

At this point things looked pretty bleak for the Allied, or "good" side. The last bastion of goodness was Great Britain, a feisty, plucky little island in the North Atlantic led by Prime Minister Winston Churchill, who had won the respect and loyalty of the British people for his ability to come up with clever insults at dinner parties. For example, there was the famous one where this woman says to him, "Lord Churchill, you're drunk!" And he replies, "Madam, I may be drunk, but BLEAAARRRGGGHHH" all over her evening gown. Churchill used this gift of eloquence to rally his countrymen when Britain was down to a three-day supply of pluck and a German invasion appeared imminent. "We shall fight them on the beaches," he said. "We shall fight them in the streets, and in the alleys, and in those things where it's like a dead end, only there's

like a circle at the end, you know? Cul somethings.''
Thus inspired, the British persevered, but by 1941 it was clear that they could not hold out long without military support from the United States. At the time Americans were strongly opposed to becoming directly involved, but that was to change drastically on the fateful December morning of October 8, when the Japanese, implementing a complex, long-term, and ultimately successful strategy to dominate the U.S. consumer-electronics market, attacked Pearl Harbor. And so it was time to have

WORLD WAR II

The best evidence we have of what World War II was like comes from about 300 million movies made during this era, many of them featuring Ronald Reagan. From these we learn that the war was fought by small groups of men, called "units," with each unit consisting of:

- One Italian person
- One Jewish person
- One Southern person
- One Tough but Caring Sergeant,[1] and of course
- One African-American.

These men often fought together through an entire double feature, during which they would

[1]Played by William Bendix.

learn, despite their differing backgrounds, how to
trickle syrup from the corners of their mouths to
indicate that they had been wounded. In the actual war, of course, real blood was used. In fact,
the actual war was extremely depressing, which is
why we're going to follow our usual procedure
here and skip directly to

The Turning Point

The turning point of the war came when the Allies
were able to break the code being used by the Axis
high command. The way this happened was, a
young British intelligence officer was looking at
some captured Nazi documents, and suddenly it
hit him. "Hey!" he said. "This is written in *German*!" From that moment on, it was only a matter
of time before June 1944, which was when the
schedule called for the Normandy Invasion. The
Germans knew it was coming, but they didn't
know where; thus it was that when, on the morning of October 8, thousands of ships disgorged
tens of thousands of troops on the beaches of Normandy, the Germans felt pretty stupid. "So *that's*
why they were calling it the 'Normandy Invasion'!" they said.[2] Stunned by this blow, the Germans began a slow, bloody retreat before the
forces of General George C. Scott, and within
months the Americans had liberated France,
whose people continue until this day to show their

---

[2] In German.

gratitude to American visitors by looking at us as though we are total Piltdown men when we try to order food.

The Final Stages of the War

America entered the final stages of the war under the leadership of Roosevelt's successor, Harry S Truman, a feisty, plucky little island in the North Atlantic, who . . . No, excuse us, we mean: a feisty, plucky native of Missouri (the "Sho' Nuff" State) who grew up so poor that his family could not afford to put a period after his middle initial, yet who went on to become a failed haberdasher. It was Truman who made the difficult decision to drop the first atomic bomb on the Japanese city of Hiroshima, the rationale being that only such a devastating, horrendous display of destructive power would convince Japan that it had to surrender. Truman also made the decision to drop the second atomic bomb on Nagasaki, the rationale being that, hey, we had another bomb.

When the war finally ended, Truman shrewdly realized that it was time to enter the Postwar Era. His first order of business was to work with the leaders of the other devastated and war-weary nations to establish some kind of mechanism to guarantee that there would be lasting world peace for a couple of months while everybody developed better weapons. It was this idealistic hope that gave birth to a noble organization that has survived and flourished to this day, an organization that affords an opportunity for representatives of virtually every nation on the globe to gather together for the purpose of freely and openly using their diplomatic license plates to violate New York City parking regulations. We refer, of course, to

THE UNITED NATIONS

The U.N. consists of two main bodies:

The General Assembly, which is, in the generous spirit of the U.N. Charter, open to just about every little dirtbag nation in the world. It has no power. Its functions are to: (1) Have formal receptions; (2) Listen to the Grateful Dead on headphones; and (3) Denounce Israel for everything, including sunspots.

The Security Council, which is limited to nations that have mastered the concept of plumbing. It is very powerful. Its functions are to: (1) Pass sweeping resolutions intended to end bloody conflicts; and then (2) Veto, ignore, or walk out on these resolutions.

But despite the presence of this potent force for peace, trouble was looming between the United States and the Soviet Union. Indeed, even as the final battles of World War II were still being fought, the battle lines were being drawn for yet another struggle—an epic struggle between the archenemy ideologies of communism and capitalism; a struggle that was to take many forms and erupt in many places; a struggle that threatened, and continues to threaten, the very survival of life on the planet; a struggle that has come to be known as

THE HAWLEY-SMOOT TARIFF

No! Sorry! That's *it* for the Hawley-Smoot Tariff; you have our word. The struggle we are referring to is of course the Cold War, which we will cover in extreme detail in the next chapter, but first let's pause for this:

TRICK DISCUSSION QUESTION

1. What did the "S" in Harry S Truman's name stand for? *(Hint: "Lucille")*

CHAPTER SEVENTEEN

International Tension City

THE END OF World War II brought an economic boom to America, as factories that had been cranking out tanks and planes for the war effort were suddenly free to produce for Mr. and Mrs. Joe Consumer.[1] This made for some pretty exciting times, because Mr. and Mrs. Consumer had very little experience with tanks and planes, and sometimes tempers would fray in traffic. ("Hey, that's *my* parking space!" "Oh yeah?" "Look out! He's turning his turret!!" "Ka-BLAMMM!!!" "AIEEEEEEE . . .")

But while things were doing well on the domes-

[1] Not their real name. Their real name was Mr. and Mrs. Bob Consumer.

tic front, problems were looming on the international front in the form of

THE COLD WAR

The Cold War gets its name from the fact that it was formed first in the Soviet Union, also known as the "U.S.S.R." or simply the "Union of the Society of Socialistic Soviet Union Communist Russians." The Soviet Union had actually been our *ally* during World War II, although today many people do not realize this, in large part because we forgot to mention it in the last chapter.

What caused the Cold War? Why did two nations that had both spilt so much blood in a common cause suddenly become archenemies? And how come it's acceptable to write "spilt"? We don't write: "I was truly thrill when the service-station attendant filt up my car with gasoline," do we? Of course not! There *are* no service-station attendants anymore! This is just one of the grim realities that we have been forced to learn to live with in the Cold War era. But what—we are going to finish this paragraph if it kills us— caused this to come about? Respected historians agree that many complex and subtly interrelated factors were involved, which is why we never sit next to historians at parties.

Speaking of parties, the Soviet Union at this time was being run by the Communists, a group of men fierce in their dedication to wearing hilariously bad suits. Their leader was Josef Stalin (Russian for "Joey Bananas"), who had risen quickly through the party ranks on the basis of possessing a high level of personal magnetism, as measured in armed henchpersons.

Stalin's strategy at the end of World War II was to acquire a small "buffer zone" between Russia and Germany, consisting of Estonia, Latvia, Lithuania, Poland, Czechoslovakia, Hungary, Romania, Bulgaria, Yugoslavia, Albania, and most of Germany. In an effort to garner public support in these nations, Stalin mounted a public-relations campaign built around the upbeat theme "Maybe We Won't Have Your Whole Family Shot," and in 1945 Eastern Europe decided to join the Communist bloc by a vote of 28,932,084,164,504,029–0. Heartened by this mandate, Stalin immediately ordered construction work to begin on the Iron Curtain, which was given its name by Sir Winston Churchill, who, in a historic anecdote at a dinner party, said: "Madam, I may be drunk, but an iron curtain has descended upon BLEAAARRRGGGHHH."

Alarmed by these prophetic words, the United States joined with eleven other nations to form the North American Treaty Organization, or UNICEF. Under this treaty, the United States agreed to station tens of thousands of troops in Western Europe. In return, the Western Europeans agreed to station tens of thousands of *their* troops in Iowa, but after a couple of weeks they got bored and went home to make imported cars. (Our troops are still over there; we keep trying to get them back, but they like the beer.) And thus the Cold War continued to deepen and broaden and widen and become larger, and by 1948 it became clear that some kind of confrontation was inevitable, and so the two superpowers decided to hold one.

The Berlin Crisis

The Berlin Crisis was caused when Stalin, encouraged by the success of his Iron Curtain, decided to set up a blockade cutting off the West's land access to West Berlin, a city that was on the good side in the Cold War but that was located, due to computer error, some 120 miles (325 kilograms) (30936.54 hectares) (2,342,424,323.3432 millipedes) *behind* the Curtain. As food supplies ran low, it began to appear as though the Berliners, despite the fact that they were feisty and of course plucky, would be starved into surrender. Just then,[2] President Truman had an idea, an idea that showed the kind of straightforward, nononsense, homespun wisdom that had served him so well in the past. "Let's drop an atomic bomb on Japan," he said. His aides, however, detected several flaws in this plan, so instead Truman decided to proceed with:

[2]October 8.

THE BERLIN AIRLIFT

This was one of the most dramatic feats in the history of dramatic aviation feats. Day after day, around the clock, U.S. planes took off from West Germany, carrying thousands of tons of clothing, medicine, fuel, and food destined for besieged Berlin. It was a stirring sight indeed to watch these mighty aircraft sweep over the surrounded city and open their cargo doors, allowing the life-giving supplies to hurtle majestically toward the grateful Berliners below. Individual cans of Spam were clocked at upward of 130 miles per hour. Despite the casualties, it was a triumph of the "can-do" American spirit, and when Truman threatened to escalate the relief effort by having the planes fly over Soviet territory and drop huge amounts of cafeteria-grade ravioli or even—remember, these were desperate times—*fruitcake,* Stalin had no choice but to call off the blockade.

But it was clear by now that communism would continue to be a serious threat abroad, and it was equally evident that the only intelligent way for Americans to deal with it was to develop a firm yet cautious and intelligent policy, based on a realistic assessment of the situation rather than blind hatred, uncontrolled emotion, and shrill accusation. Still, that seemed like an awful lot of work, so instead we had

The Red Scare

The Scare was started by Joseph McCarthy, who was a senator from Wisconsin. That's the strange thing about Wisconsin: You think of it as being this nice friendly state full of decent, God-fearing, cow-oriented people, and here they elect this vicious alcoholic psychopathic lunatic. And it's not just an isolated incident: In recent years, Wisconsin has also attempted to elect Charles Manson, Hermann Göring, Jabba the Hutt, and, chillingly, Geraldo Rivera. We think it's something in the cheese.

Anyway, McCarthy made a series of speeches in which he charged that Communists had infiltrated the federal government to the point where the State Department had an actual Communist dining room, Communist men's bowling team, and so forth. At first, skeptics scoffed at these charges, but when McCarthy produced solid evidence in the form of a piece of paper that appeared, at least from a distance, to have something written on it, the press, displaying the kind of journalistic integrity that we normally associate only with restroom bacteria, had no choice but to print the story, and the Scare was on.

Speaking of bacteria, a highly active Communist-finder during this era was a young attorney named Richard "Dick" Milhous "Milhous" Nixon, who had gotten elected to Congress from a California district despite the handicap that he re-

minded people of a nocturnal rodent. It was Nixon
who nailed proven suspected Communist and Red
Fellow Traveler Alger Hiss, the turning point in
the case coming when Nixon, accompanied by reporters, went to a Maryland farm, where he
reached into a hollowed-out pumpkin and, in a moment of high drama, pulled out a cocker spaniel
named Checkers. This was widely believed to be
the end of his career. (Nixon's.)

Eventually the public came to its senses and the
Red Scare hysteria died down, and today, thank
goodness, we no longer see politicians attempting
to gain power by accusing their opponents of
being unpatriotic, except during elections. Speaking of which, we almost forgot to mention the dramatic

1948 PRESIDENTIAL ELECTION

In 1948 the Democrats had little choice but to
nominate President Truman, under the banner
HE'S GOING TO LOSE. Everybody felt this way: the
politicians, the press, the pollsters, the piccolo
players, Peter Piper, everybody. The Republicans
were so confident that they nominated an individual named Thomas Dewey, whose lone accomplishment was inventing the decimal system. Truman
campaigned doggedly around the nation, but his
cause appeared to be hopeless. A Dewey victory
seemed so inevitable that on election night, the

Chicago Tribune printed the famous front-page headline DEWEY DEFEATS TRUMAN. This was because Dewey *had* defeated Truman, who immediately threatened to drop an atomic bomb on Chicago, so everybody went ha-ha-ha-ha, just kidding, and wisely elected to let the feisty ex-haberdasher have another term.

This was typical of the carefree attitude widespread in the nation during the postwar years. Popular culture saw millions of "bobby soxers"[3] swooning over a feisty, skinny crooner named Frank Sinatra, while young "hep cats" wore "zoot suits," and danced the "jitterbug" to "platters" on the "jukebox." In short, the whole nation was behaving like "dorks," and it was only a matter of time before some kind of terrible event occurred.

THE KOREAN WAR

The Korean War was, as is so often the case with wars, not especially amusing, except for those soldiers who were fortunate enough to get in a fun unit featuring Alan Alda and a host of wacky and zany characters and young nurses with terrific bodies. So we're going to continue our policy of skipping over the depressing parts and hasten ahead to the fifties, although we would like to

[3]Not their real names.

"toot our own horn" just a little bit here and point out that we have managed to get through this entire chapter without once mentioning

THE H*****-S**** T*****

If you get our drift.

DISCUSSION QUESTIONS

1. Remember when the United States was supposed to switch over to the metric system, and the federal government put up road signs in kilometers, and in some areas people actually *shot the signs down*? Wasn't that *great*?
2. Do you think "Checkers" is a good name for a dog? What about "Booger"? Explain.

EXTRA-CREDIT PROJECT

Think of a joke that starts this way:
  "Knock knock."
  "Who's there?"
  "Lithuania."
  (Hint: This joke could involve lisping.)

CHAPTER EIGHTEEN

The Fifties:
Peace, Prosperity,
Brain Death

BECAUSE OF scheduling problems, the fifties did not officially begin until 1952. This, coincidentally, was the year of the 1952 presidential election campaign, in which both parties, recognizing that the nation was locked into a deadly Cold War struggle, when the slightest mistake could mean the destruction of the entire planet, nominated bald men with silly names. The Democrats went with Adlai Stevenson, a suspected intellectual, and the Republicans went with Dwight "David" Eisenhower, who was extremely popular for winning World War II and having the likable nickname "Ike," which he got from a sound that his friend Sir Winston Churchill made just before pitching face-first into his food at a dinner party.

Going into the race, Eisenhower had a strong
tactical advantage stemming from the fact that
nobody, including himself, knew what his views
were. But his campaign quickly became enmeshed
in scandal when it was discovered that his running
mate, Senator "Dick" Nixon, had received money
from a secret fund. Realizing that his career was
at stake, Nixon appeared on a live television
broadcast and told the American people, with deep
emotion in his voice, that if they didn't let him be
the vice president, he would kill his dog. This was
widely believed to be the end of his career.

Nevertheless, Eisenhower, buoyed by the inspirational and deeply meaningful campaign theme
"I like Ike," won the election and immediately
plunged into an ambitious and arduous schedule
that often involved playing golf and taking a nap
on the same day. This resulted in a humongous economic boom that caused millions of Americans to
purchase comically styled big cars and hightail it
to the suburbs. Thus began a Golden Era in this
country that is still looked back upon with nostalgia by the millions of Americans who are involved
in the manufacture and sale of nostalgia-related
products.

CULTURE IN THE FIFTIES

The fifties were an extremely important cultural
era, because this was the phase when the postwar

"Baby Boom" generation grew up, and we Boomers are quite frankly fascinated with anything involving ourselves. Like, when we started having our own babies, it was all we could talk about for *years*. We went around describing our child-having and child-rearing experiences in breathtaking detail, as though the rest of you had no experience whatsoever in these fields. We're sorry if you find all this boring, but it's not *our* fault that you were not fortunate enough to have been born into such an intriguing and important generation. We can only imagine how interesting we are going to be at cocktail parties when we start getting into death.

But back to the fifties: The best archival source for accurate information about life during this era is the brilliant TV documentary series *Ozzie and Harriet*. From this we learn that the fifties were a time when once per week some kind of epochal crisis would occur, such as Ricky borrowing David's sweater without asking, and it would take a half an hour to resolve this crisis, owing to the fact that the male head of household had the IQ of dirt. But other than that, life was very good, considering it was filmed in black and white.

Another important television show of the era was *The Mickey Mouse Club,* which made enormous cultural contributions, by which we mean: Annette Funicello. Annette had a *major* impact on many of us male Baby Boomers, especially the part where she came marching out wearing a T-shirt with her name printed on it, and some of the letters were considerably closer to the camera than others. If you get our drift.

But the most truly wonderful fifties show was *Queen for a Day,* starring Your Host, Jack Bailey. This was a kind of Game Show from Hell where three women competed to see who had the most miserable life. We are not making this show up. Contestant Number One would say something like, "Well, I have terminal cancer, of course, and little Billy's iron lung was destroyed in the fire, and . . ." and so on. Everybody in the audience would be weeping, and then Contestant Number Two would tell a story that was even *worse.* And then Contestant Number Three would make the other two sound like Mary Poppins. After which Jack Bailey would have the members of the audience clap to show which woman they thought was the most wretched, and she would receive some very nice gifts including (always) an Amana freezer. It was fabulous television, and a nice freezer, and it remained unsurpassed until three decades later, with the emergence—probably as a result of toxic waste in the water supply—of Geraldo Rivera.

Of course television was not the only cultural contribution of the fifties. There was also the Hula-Hoop, and Marlon Brando. And let's not forget the interstate highway system, which made it possible for a family to hop into a car in Cleveland, and a little over four hours later, find themselves still delayed by road construction just outside of Cleveland. We are still benefiting from this system.

But the significant cultural innovation of the fifties was musical—a new "sound" called "rock 'n' roll," an exciting, high-energy style of music that, in its raucous disregard for the gentler, more complacent tastes of an older generation, reflected the young people's growing disillusionment with the stultifying, numbing, bourgeois, and materialistic values of an increasingly homogeneous society through such lyrics as:

> *Bomp ba ba bomp*
> *Ba bomp ba bomp bomp*
> *A dang a dang dang*
> *A ding a dong ding,*
> *Blue moon.*

Of the many legendary rock "performers" to emerge during this era—"Fats" Checker, the Pylons, the Gol-Darnits, Buster and the Harpoons, Bill Hawley and the Smoots, and so on—the greatest of them all was "The King," Elvis Presley, who went on to become the largest (Ha-ha![1]) record-seller of all time, and who is to this very day sometimes seen shopping in rural supermarkets.

So there's no question about it: By the mid-fifties, America was definitely in a Golden Era, an era of excitement and opportunity for all citizens, regardless of race or creed or color, unless the

[1]Get it?

color happened to be black. Then there was a problem. Because at the time the nation was functioning under the racial doctrine of "Separate but Equal," which got its name from the fact that black people were required to use *separate* facilities that were *equal* to the facilities that white people kept for their domestic animals. This system had worked for many decades, and nobody saw any real reason to change until one day in 1954 when a group of outside agitators arrived from outer space to file a suit against the Topeka, Kansas, Board of Education. This led to the historic and just Supreme Court ruling, a landmark, that *nobody,* black or white, should have to go to school in Topeka, Kansas. Thus was born the civil rights movement, an epic struggle that has required much sacrifice and pain, but which has enabled the United States to progress, in just three decades, from being a nation where blacks were forced to ride in the back of the bus, to being a nation where, due to federal cutbacks, there *is* no bus.

THE PRESIDENTIAL ELECTION
OF 1956

Things were going so smoothly at this point that the voters didn't really feel like going through a whole new presidential election, so they decided to hold the 1952 election over again, and it came out the same. In a word, everything seemed to be working out very well, and the fifties would probably have been pure perfection except that—it seems like this *always* happens—all these pesky foreign affairs kept occurring in the form of crises, starting with

THE SUEZ CRISIS

This crisis involved the Suez Canal, which was built by the French ("Suez!" is the word used to call French pigs[2]) and which is extremely strategic because it is the only navigable water route connecting the Red Sea with Albany, New York. Hence, you can imagine how tense the world became on the morning of October 8 when this area became the scene of a full-blown crisis, although we cannot for the life of us remember what the hell it was. But we're fairly sure it's over. You never hear about it on the news.

At around this same time a number of other international crises, most of them also fully blown, occurred in Hungary, Poland, Lebanon, and the quiz-show industry. But all of these paled by comparison to

THE *SPUTNIK* CRISIS

One day in 1957 everybody in the United States was minding his or her own business when sud-

[2]Not that they come.

denly the Russians launched a grapefruit-size object called *Sputnik* (literally, "Little Sput") into an Earth orbit, from which it began transmitting back the following potentially vital intelligence information (and we quote): *"Beep."* This came as a severe shock to Americans, because at that point the best our space scientists had been able to come up with was a walnut-size object that went: *"Moo."* And thus began the Space Race, which was to have an enormous worldwide impact on Mrs. DeLucia's fifth-grade class, which was where we were at the time. All of a sudden Mrs. DeLucia was telling us we were going to have to study a LOT more science and math, including such concepts as the "cosine." As if the whole thing were *our* fault.

So it was a difficult time, but by 1960 the nation was starting to feel a little better. "Well," we said brightly in unison, "at least there haven't been any crises for a while!" Which was of course the signal for the International Crisis Promotion Council to swing into action and produce:

THE U-2 CRISIS

This crisis occurred when the Russians shot down an American U-2 reconnaissance plane flying deep into their airspace, and then accused us—this is the kind of paranoid thinking that makes the Russians so untrustworthy—of conducting aerial reconnaissance. Our government offered a number of highly plausible and perfectly innocent explanations for the flight, such as:

- It was a weather plane.
- It was a traffic plane.
- It was swamp gas.
- The dog ate our homework.

But eventually, President Eisenhower, emerging from a high-level nap, was forced to admit that it was in fact a spy plane, at which point the Russians, led by Nikita "The Human Potato" Khrushchev, stomped out of the Paris summit conference before the appetizers had even arrived, leaving "Ike" with nobody to negotiate with except himself. And although he won several major concessions, the feeling was becoming widespread among the American people that maybe it was time for a change—time to get some "new blood" in the White House and "get the country moving again." And it just so happened that at that very moment, a new "star" was rising on the public scene—a young man whose boyish good looks, energy, quick wit, and graceful charm would soon capture the hearts of the nation and even the world: Pat Boone. Or maybe that was 1955.

DISCUSSION QUESTIONS

1. Do you think we've had enough Winston Churchill jokes? Explain.

2. Have you, or has anybody you have ever met, ever found *any* use for the cosine? We didn't think so.

EXTRA CREDIT

Try to think up a campaign slogan even more inane than "I like Ike." *(Hint: This is not possible.)*

BONUS QUESTION

What does one *do* with extra credit, anyway?

CHAPTER NINETEEN

The Sixties:
A Nation Gets High and
Has Amazing Insights,
Many of Which Later On Turn Out
to Seem Kind of Stupid

THE SIXTIES was a unique era in American history. Mention the sixties to any middle-aged urban professional, and he'll transform himself into something worse than one of those Depressionites, droning away about his memories until you think up an excuse to leave. Such is the impact that this exciting era still has on the American consciousness. Because it was a time of truth, but also of lies; of love, but also of hate; of peace, but also of war; of Otis Redding, but also of Sonny Bono. There was a "new feeling" in the land, especially among the young people, who joined the "hippie movement" to express their need to be free, to challenge the traditional values of American culture, to order some pizza *right now.* Yes, the "times they were a-changin'," and nobody expressed the spirit of the sixties better than the brilliant young poet-songwriter-irritatingly-nasal-whiner Bob Dylan, when, with his usual insightfulness, he sang:

> *How many times can a man be a man*
> *Before a man is a man?*

Moved by the power of this message, tens of thousands of young people rejected the trappings of a grasping greedy society to live simple, uncluttered lives dedicated to meditation and spirituality and listening to sitar music and ingesting random substances and becoming intensely interested in the ceiling and driving home at one mile per hour. As a result of these experiences, the "Flower Children" of the sixties developed a unique set of values, a strong sense of idealism and social awareness that still exerts a powerful influence over their decisions in such philosophical areas as what radio stations to listen to when driving their Jaguars to their brokerage firms.

THE 1960 PRESIDENTIAL ELECTION

In 1960 the Democratic candidate was the rich witty graceful charming and of course boyishly handsome Massachusetts senator John Fitzgerald Kennedy, who gained voter recognition by having his face on millions of souvenir plates and being married to the lovely and internationally admired Jacqueline Kennedy Onassis. Kennedy's major political drawback was that the nation had never elected a Roman Catholic; on the other hand, the nation had never elected a total dweeb, either, and the Republicans had for some reason nominated "Dick" Nixon. So it was a very close race.

The turning point was a series of nationally televised debates, in which Kennedy, who looked tanned and relaxed, seemed to have an advantage over Nixon, who looked as though he had been coached by ferrets. Kennedy held a slight lead going into the bonus round, where he chose Category Three (Graceful Handsome Boyish Wittiness) and won the matching luggage *plus* Texas *plus* Illinois, thus guaranteeing his victory in the November election. This was widely believed to be the end of Nixon's career.

THE KENNEDY ADMINISTRATION

Kennedy had pledged, during the 1960 election campaign, to "get the country moving again"—to get it out of the Eisenhower doldrums, to bring back its vigor, to reinstill its pride, to reassert its leadership around the world, maybe even to get it into a dumbfounding, unwinnable war. And under the gracefully boyishly handsomely witty charmingness of his leadership, America began to do just that. Kennedy immediately set the tone in his inaugural address, in which he promised that the country would land a Peace Corps volunteer on the Moon, and ended with the stirring words of the famous challenge "Ask not what your country cannot do that *you* cannot do, nor what cannot be done by neither you *nor* your country, whichever is greater."

The Kennedys also captivated the nation with their unique "style," which soon earned the young administration the nickname "Camelot" (from the popular Broadway musical *Guys and Dolls*). The Kennedy style was an eclectic blend of amusing and graceful activities that ranged from taking fifty-mile hikes to inviting cellist Pablo Casals to perform at the White House to playing touch football on the lawn. As the Kennedy mystique grew, the first family's activities were widely imitated: Before long, millions of Americans were taking Pablo Casals on fifty-mile hikes. When he begged for a chance to rest, they laughed and threw footballs at him. Such was the vigor of the times.

So everything would probably have been ideal if the Red Communists had not decided to be their usual party-pooper selves by causing new international tension in the form of

The Bay of Pigs

In 1960 there was considerable concern about the fact that Fidel Castro, a known beard-wearing Communist, had taken over Cuba, which is a mere

ninety miles from Key West, Florida, site of
America's largest strategic stockpile of tasteless
T-shirts. This alarmed the U.S. intelligence community, whose crack team of analysts developed a
shrewd plan under which the U.S. would secretly
train an army to invade Cuba; which then, according to the plan, would cause the population to rise
up in revolt and throw Castro out of power. This
plan worked smoothly, with everything going exactly as planned, except the part about the population rising up in revolt, and so forth. It turned
out that large segments of the population had *already* risen up in revolt just a short time earlier to
put Castro *into* power, but unfortunately our intelligence community had misplaced the file folder
containing this tidbit of information. So the invasion failed and the U.S. got some international
egg on its face. But Kennedy took it with his
usual boyishly witty graceful handsome charming-
hood, and the intelligence community, showing ad-
mirable spunk, quickly discovered an exciting new
place to think up shrewd plans about: Southeast
Asia.

Once more everything seemed to be going pretty
well, until, wouldn't you know it, along came

The Berlin Crisis

This was caused when the Russians noticed that
every morning approximately 173,000 East Berlin
residents commuted to work in West Berlin, and
every evening approximately 8 of them commuted

back. The Russians, showing the kind of subtle public-relations skills that have made them so popular everywhere they tromp, responded by building the Berlin Wall, which created a crisis that was not resolved until President Kennedy went over there in person and made the famous inspirational proclamation *"Ich bin ein Berliner"* ("I wish to see a menu"). This calmed international tensions, but only briefly, for in October 1962 a major event was to occur, an event that would become the focus of the world's attention for several tense days. We refer, of course, to the World Series, in which the Yankees beat the Giants four games to three. Also, there was a Cuban missile crisis, which the United States won in the final minutes by going into a "prevent" defense.

Another shocking development that occurred at this time was that "Dick" Nixon reached such a low level of credibility with the voters that *even California refused to elect him as governor.* In his concession speech, Nixon told the press: "You won't have Dick Nixon to kick around anymore," prompting the reporters, in a fit of nostalgia, to batter him unconscious with their wingtips. This was widely believed to be the end of his career.

So by 1963, all things considered, the sixties seemed to be going pretty well. Which just goes to show that you can never tell, because except for the discovery of Aretha Franklin, the rest of the decade turned out to be

A LONG STRING OF BUMMERS

First of all, Kennedy was assassinated, which was traumatic enough in itself but was made even worse by the fact that we never did find out for sure what happened, which means that for the rest of our lives we're going to be opening *People* magazine and reading articles about yet another conspiracy buff claiming to have conclusive proof that Lee Harvey Oswald was actually working for Roy Orbison or the Nabisco Corporation or whatever.

THEN we got President Lyndon Johnson, who tried his darnedest, by means of looking somber to the point of intestinal discomfort, to convey integrity, but who nevertheless made you think immediately of the large comically dishonest Warner Brothers cartoon rooster Foghorn Leghorn. Plus his wife—this is still difficult to believe, even years later—was named "Lady Bird." Johnson was nevertheless elected overwhelmingly in 1964, easily defeating Republican nominee Barry Goldwater, who turned out to be an OK guy but who at the time appeared to be perfectly likely to launch a nuclear first strike against, say, New York.

THEN we got into the Vietnam War, which is *still* causing arguments involving:

- the people who supported it but didn't fight in it, versus
- the people who didn't support it but did fight in it, versus

- the people who didn't support it *and* didn't fight in it, versus
- the people who supported it and *might* have had to fight in it if ever the Indiana National Guard had been called up, which was of course a distinct possibility,

and so on.

THEN more people got assassinated and everybody started hating everybody and there were riots in the streets.

THEN *Gilligan's Island* was canceled.

So by 1968 things were really bad. They were so bad that it seemed impossible for them to get any worse, unless something truly horrible happened, something so twisted and sinister and evil that the human mind could barely comprehend it.

THE NIXON COMEBACK

Yes. One day we turned on our televisions, and there he was, "Dick" Nixon, looking stronger than ever despite the holes in his suit where various stakes had been driven into his heart. He was advertised as a "new" Nixon with all kinds of amazing features, including an illuminated glove compartment and a secret plan to end the war in Vietnam, but of course he couldn't tell the voters what it was, because then it wouldn't have been a *secret* plan.

Nixon's running mate was an individual named Spiro Agnew, whose principal qualification was that when you rearranged the letters of his name, you got "grow a penis."[1] Their campaign theme— we are not making this up—was "Law and Order."

The Democrats, meanwhile, were in trouble. The war had become extremely unpopular, so President Johnson had decided not to seek reelection, which was an act of great statesmanship in the sense that nobody except maybe Lady Bird would have voted for him anyway. The process by which the Democrats decided who would be their new nominee was about as organized as a tub of live bait, culminating in the 1968 Chicago convention, which consisted of spokespersons for about 253 major ideological factions giving each other the finger through clouds of tear gas. Out of this process emerged Hubert Humphrey, a nice man with a lot of solid experience and an unfortunate tendency to sound like Porky Pig, only not as dignified. On top of this, the Democrats had to contend with the candidacy of Alabama governor George Wallace, who appealed to what the political experts called "disaffected Democrats," defined as "Democrats missing key teeth."

And thus it was that on election day, October 8, 1968, the voters went to the polls and elected, as

[1]Dick Cavett discovered this. Really.

leader of the greatest nation that the world has
ever seen, President Richard Milhous N . . .

President Richard M . . .

President R . . .

Please don't make us do this.

THE NIXON PRESIDENCY

Nixon's first official act as president was to sneak
out behind the White House and bury his secret
peace plan to ensure that nobody would find out
what it was, which would have been a breach of
national security. With that important task accomplished, he swung into action, working fever-
ishly to accomplish his most important objective,
to realize the cherished dream that had driven him
through all these years of disappointment, to
reach the long-sought goal that, thanks to his election, was finally within his grasp, namely: getting
reelected.

DISCUSSION QUESTIONS

1. Didn't you always, even when you were sitting around
   with your friends pretending to be really enthralled, secretly *hate* sitar music? Admit it.

CHAPTER TWENTY

The Seventies: A Relieved Nation Learns That It Does Not Actually *Need* a President

THE SEVENTIES dawned with "Dick" Nixon riding high. The nation had surged ahead in the space race through a series of courageous accomplishments by astronauts such as Donald "Deke" Slayton, Edwin "Buzz" Aldrin, Scott "Scotty" Carpenter, and Nicholas "Nicky the Squid" Calamari, climaxing with the historic moment on October 8 when Neil "Satchmo" Armstrong became the first human, with the possible exception of guitarist Jimi Hendrix, to set foot on the Moon, where he expressed the emotions of an anxiously watching world with the unforgettable statement "Hi, Mom!"

On the foreign-policy front, Nixon continued to protect the national security by not telling anybody, not even his secret wife, Pat, what his secret plan to end the Vietnam War was. At the same time, he undertook a major clandestine foreign-policy initiative by sending chocolates and long-stemmed roses to legendary Communist Chinese revolutionary leader Mao ("Mo the Dong") Zedong. Helping him with this initiative was the brilliant, avocado-shaped genius Henry Kissinger, who became the nation's top foreign-policy strategist despite being born with the handicaps of a laughable accent and no morals or neck.

The daring initiative came to fruition in 1972 when Nixon became the first American president to visit China, where Mao, an avid prankster, presented him with two giant pandas, named Ling-Ling and Hsing-Hsing. This was actually a hilarious Communist joke, because "Ling-Ling" and "Hsing-Hsing" are the words that Chinese children use to describe bodily outputs, as in "Mommy, I have to make ling-ling." The Chinese officials just about died laughing when Nixon was making his thank-you speech and Ling-Ling went hsing-hsing on his shoe. (The pandas now reside in the National Zoo, where, over the past eighteen years, nearly a third of the federal budget has been spent on various elaborate schemes to get them to reproduce, which is also pretty funny inasmuch as they are both males.)

The China initiative was a notable coup, and even though the darned pesky Vietnam War was still going on, everybody knew that "Dick" had his secret plan, which he could dig up and put into effect at any time. So things looked very good indeed for him going into the 1972 election. He got a lot of help from the Democrats, who, continuing the tradition they established in 1968 of appearing to be incapable of operating an electric blanket, let alone the country, nominated George McGovern, who had exhibited a wide-ranging appeal to a broad cross section of nearly fourteen voters. The result was that in the 1972 election Nixon carried all the states and every major planet except Massachusetts.

So by 1973 "Dick" Nixon was at the pinnacle of power and appeared poised to become, against all odds, one of the most successful and respected presidents in the nation's history. This was the signal for God to come into the game and create

THE WATERGATE SCANDAL

The Watergate Scandal, which gets its name from the fact that it was a scandal, began with a break-in of the Democratic National Committee headquarters by a group of burglars so ludicrously incompetent that they obviously had to have some connection with the federal government. Sure enough, when two plucky and persistent *Washington Post* reporters, played by Robert Redford and Dustin Hoffman, began poking around, a confidential source named "Deep Throat"—whose identity remains a closely guarded secret to this very

day because it was Pat Nixon in drag—revealed to
them a fascinating tidbit of information: *Some spe-
cies of mollusk can actually change their gender.*

This was the "missing puzzle piece" that the
two brash young journalists needed to "break the
story." Within days the scandal was such hot
news that it was turned into a highly popular television series called *The Senate Watergate Committee's Parade of Scuzzballs,* starring genial host
"Senator Sam" Ervin (D-Okeefenokee), who had
the entire nation listening with rapt attention in
an effort to figure out what the hell he was saying.
Senator Sam spoke in Deep Southern, which is
similar to English, only unintelligible, so everything he said came out sounding like "We go' hep-
pin' wif de bane pone." But everybody was on his
side anyway, because the committee witnesses—a
group of high-level Nixon administration aides, all
of them named Klaus—projected all the warmth
and personal integrity of eels. (We are pleased to
report, however, that while in federal prison they
all found the Lord, who was serving a six-year
sentence for failing to file tax returns.)

So things looked very bad for the Nixon administration, and they got even worse with the revelation that Nixon had secretly taped all the Oval
Office conversations that had taken place between
him and the various Klauses. The tapes contained
many shocking and highly revealing exchanges,
such as this one, from October 8:

NIXON: Because you have, you have problems with
the, with the [expletive deleted], with the . . .
KLAUS: Yeah [garbled], with the, uh, with the . . .
NIXON: . . . with, uh, with the [expletive deleted].
KLAUS: . . . with the . . .
NIXON: [Expletive deleted].
KLAUS: . . . with the Smoot-Hawley.
NIXON: Shit.

As damaging as these revelations were, matters
got even worse for Nixon when one of the tapes
was found to contain, at a crucial juncture, an
eighteen-minute gap where nothing could be heard
except a hum. This was the last straw: The American public simply would not tolerate a president
who would fritter away eighteen minutes hum-
ming during a crucial juncture. The next day, October 8, the Senate Watergate Committee voted
17–9 in favor of a resolution proposed by Senator
Ervin calling on the president to "Rang onsum
latmun sookles." Clearly the dice had been cast
down onto the gauntlet. Nixon appeared to have
only two options left:

- OPTION ONE: He could boldly remain as president and defend himself in the now-inevitable
  impeachment proceedings.
- OPTION TWO: He could spare the country further trauma by resigning in a dignified manner.

Those of you who are well-schooled students of
"Dick" Nixon will not be surprised to learn that,

after carefully weighing the alternatives, he decided to go with Option Three: to stand in the Rose Garden and make a semicoherent speech about his mother that may well rank as the single most embarrassing moment in American history. Thoroughly humiliated, Nixon then went off to live in a state of utter disgrace.[1] This was widely believed to be the end of his career.

Nixon's resignation left the nation in shock, compounded when enterprising *Washington Post* reporters revealed that, while nobody was paying attention, Vice President Agnew had resigned to take a job clubbing baby seals. This meant that the new president of the United States was—this all seems like a dream now—*Gerald Ford.* Yes! The golf person!

HIGHLIGHTS OF
THE FORD ADMINISTRATION

The major highlight was when Ford gave Nixon a full presidential pardon, thereby sparing the nation the trauma of seeing "Dick" go to federal prison, where there was every reason to fear that he would—this makes us shudder just thinking about it—find the Lord. Ford also restored the nation's respect for the office of the presidency by falling down and bonking his head a lot.

Another major Ford highlight was when he

[1] New Jersey.

alerted the nation that there was going to be an epidemic of "swine flu" and that everybody should get a shot. As it turned out, there was less of a risk from the disease than from the shots, but fortunately only a few high-level administration officials were dumb enough to get them.

Of course there were many other Ford administration highlights, but unfortunately we lost the matchbook we had them written on. Your best bet, if you want more information on this topic, is to visit the official Gerald R. Ford Presidential Museum in Grand Rapids, Michigan, which features, among other fascinating exhibits, all of the former chief executive's merit badges.[2]

So Ford made an important contribution as a "caretaker" president, but by the time the 1976 election rolled around, America was ready to turn in an entirely new direction for leadership. America had grown deeply suspicious of establishment politicians, and wanted a different kind of president, a president who was not a Washington "insider," a president who rejected the ostentatious trappings of power, a president who was moral and decent and sensitive and kind and earnest and truthful and pious and had nice hair like Phil Donahue. America was ready to be led by: a weenie.

[2]Really.

"JIMMY" CARTER

Jimmy Carter came from a simple God-fearing homespun southern family that was normal in every respect except that many of its members, upon close inspection, appeared to be crazy. After graduating from the U.S. Naval Academy, he served as an officer aboard a nuclear submarine, where, due to an unfortunate radiation leakage, he developed enormous mutant teeth. Nevertheless he went on to become a successful peanut farmer and governor of Georgia for an entire term, thus acquiring all of the major qualifications that a modern politician needs to be president of the United States, namely: blue suits. He easily won the Democratic nomination in 1976 to face Gerald Ford, who won the GOP nomination after narrowly edging out former California governor Ronald Reagan by a score of four brain cells to three.

During the election campaign, Carter performed many symbolic gestures to show he was a regular common person only much smarter. For example, he often carried his own garment bag. This impressed the voters, although it was eventually revealed by enterprising *Washington Post* reporters that the bag did not, in fact, contain a single garment. Nevertheless Carter won the election and went on to have several highlights.

HIGHLIGHTS OF THE CARTER ADMINISTRATION

The main one, without question, was when the president claimed that while he was out in a canoe one day, he was attacked by an enormous swimming rabbit. We swear we are not making this highlight up. Also there was an energy crisis during which Americans, showing the sense of self-sacrifice and community spirit that often emerges when the well-being of the nation is at stake, closed ranks and shot at each other in gas lines.

The lowlight of the Carter administration was that the economy did poorly. This troubled Jimmy a great deal, so much so that he gathered together all of the nation's top thinkers for a special conference at Camp David. They thought and thought and thought, and when they were finally done, Jimmy came out and announced that the nation's problems were being caused by "malaise." This puzzled the average American, who had never even heard of "malaise," except on a sandwich, and who was under the impression that the problem was that unemployment and inflation were running at about 652 billion percent. "Any minute now," the average American thought, "he's gonna tell us we have to get 'malaise' shots."

So there was much disillusionment among the voting public. The stage was set for yet another dramatic change in the nation's political direction, a shift away from the soul-searching, the uncertainty, the intellectual complexity, and the multisyllabic words of the Carter era; a shift toward a new kind of leader, a man with a gift for communicating the kind of clear, direct, uncomplicated message that had previously been associated only with Tide commercials. It was time for the Reagan Revolution.

DISCUSSION QUESTIONS

1. How do they know what gender a mollusk is?

CHAPTER TWENTY-ONE

The Reagan-Bush Years: Napping Toward Glory

THE 1980s will be remembered as a time when the nation broke free of the confining chains of the left-leaning bleeding-heart gutless namby-pamby Mister Pouty Pants Liberal school of political thought that had dominated the American political landscape ever since the New Deal; a time when Americans began Standing Tall, Talking Proud, Feeling Good, Sitting Straight, Pledging Allegiance, and Eating More Fiber.

Who was responsible for this sweeping change in the national mood? Amazingly, it was almost entirely the work of a single person, a strong, dominant individual who was able to change the course of history through steely determination, unflinching toughness, and sheer force of will:

Nancy Reagan. But you also have to give a lot of credit to her husband, Ron, a distinguished war-movie hero who served, off and on, as president of the United States during this era, and whose administration made many historically crucial decisions, several of which he was aware of personally.

Coinciding with this national mood change was the emergence and rapid choleralike spreading of young urban professionals, also known as "yuppies" or, more affectionately, "suspender-wearing wingtipped weenies," a new breed of seriously ambitious humanoids whose idea of a really wild evening was to get drunk and restructure a corporation. The role models for the eighties were men like Donald Trump, who had made several jillion dollars in the lucrative field of amassing wealth. But beyond being stupendously rich, Trump was also truly a class individual, as he revealed in his best-selling book, *Trump: Truly a Class Individual,* and in 1989 he captured the imagination of the nation when, in the largest private financial transaction ever, he purchased Ohio, the Coast Guard, the Italian Renaissance, and Mars.[1]

Another major trend of the 1980s was the sudden ubiquitousness of the personal computer, a tool that has freed millions of people to use words like "ubiquitousness" without actually knowing how to spell them. In fact, the book that you are

---

[1]All of which he classily renamed "Trump."

now reading was written on a personal computer, which is why it is devoid of the "typos" that were so common in the days of old-fashioned wersp oidop gfegkog pl;gpp$R$%!%.

But all was not peaches and light on the 1980s economic front. After a lengthy investigation, crack agents of the Securities and Exchange Commission discovered that top Wall Street figures were using "inside information" to make money, a revelation that came as a shock to those members of the public who had mince pie for brains. Investor confidence was further shaken by the stockmarket crash of October 8, 1987, caused by a herd of computers that were panicked into the worst international electronic stampede in history when a woman in Akron, Ohio, got angry and punched an automatic bank teller.[2]

Another major economic upheaval was the sudden end of the energy crisis, which meant lower gas prices and harder times for wealthy Texans as well as large oil companies, thereby causing alarmed, thoughtful Americans everywhere to laugh until their garments were soaked with drool. Things were also very bad for the American family farmer, whose fields, by the late 1980s, were parched and dusty because of the bright lights being shone on them by television news crews doing heartrending reports about the plight of the family farmer.

[2]Charging it later with sexual harassment.

Internationally, the major event of the eighties
was that Prince Charles married Diana Spencer,
thus assuring that they would be featured on
roughly every third cover of *People* for the rest of
our lives. But when all is said and done, which,
trust us, will be very soon now, the story of the
eighties will be the story of the Reagan administration and the many men and women who served
in it, some of whom are already out on parole.

THE 1980 PRESIDENTIAL ELECTION CAMPAIGN

In 1980 the Democrats were pretty much stuck
with Jimmy Carter and Walter Mondale, who ran
under the slogan "Four More Years?" The
Republicans, meanwhile, had a spirited primary-
campaign season, which came down to a duel between Reagan and George Herbert Walker Norris
Wainright Armoire Vestibule Pomegranate Bush
IV, who had achieved a distinguished record of
government service despite having a voice that
sounded like he had just inhaled an entire blimp-
load of helium.

Reagan finally won the nomination by promot-
ing "Reaganomics," an economic program based
on the theory that the government could *lower*
taxes while *increasing* spending and at the same
time actually *reduce* the federal budget deficit by
sacrificing a *live* chicken by the light of a *full*
moon. Bush charged that this amounted to "voo-

doo economics," which got him into hot water until he explained that what he meant to say was "doo-doo economics." Satisfied, Reagan made Bush his vice-presidential nominee.

The turning point in the election campaign came during the October 8 debate between Reagan and Carter, when Reagan's handlers came up with a shrewd strategy: No matter what Carter said, Reagan would respond by shaking his head in a sorrowful but personable manner and saying: "There you go again." This was brilliant, because (a) it required the candidate to remember only four words, and (b) he delivered them so believably that everything Carter said seemed like a lie. If Carter had stated that the Earth was round, Reagan would have shaken his head, saying, "There you go again," and millions of voters would have said: "Yeah! What does Carter think we are? *Stupid?*"

And so the Reagan-Bush juggernaut easily swept to victory in all but a handful of states,[3] thus paving the way for

THE REAGAN REVOLUTION

The Reagan Revolution was run by staunch conservatives who wanted the government to stop wasting money on bloated, inefficient social programs and start wasting it on bloated, inefficient

[3] Which were immediately purchased by Donald Trump.

military programs. Foremost among these was the Strategic Defense Initiative, or "Star Wars," which is a far-flung network of highly sophisticated, state-of-the-art "defense contractors" orbiting a giant, five-sided structure called the "Pentagon," which constantly emits high-intensity beams of "money." In the event of a nuclear attack, electronic communications devices called "telephones" would be used to instantaneously alert the president and his top "defense strategists" that it is time for them to be whisked to secret radiation-proof underground "hideouts" stocked with food and water and recreational activities such as "Ping-Pong" and protected by vicious biting dogs from intrusion by sick, desperate, starving, and increasingly hairless "taxpayers." Thanks to the miracle of computers, all this would take place in less time than it takes for a family of four to order breakfast!

However, in the area of foreign policy, the major focus of the first Reagan term was Central America, a region of immense strategic vitality to the United States because if it were to ever fall into the hands of communist troops, they would be eaten by insects. Thus it was with extreme interest that Americans viewed the struggle between the "Sandinistas," a group of anticommunist ex–military officers from Honduras, to overthrow the "contras," a group of pro-militarist ex-communists from El Salvador, in an effort to control Nicaragua, the site of the vital Suez Canal, which

. . . No, wait a minute. Sorry. What we mean is, Americans viewed with extreme interest the struggle between the "Hondurans," a group of ex-Panamanian Nicaraguans, to control the "Canal Zones," a group of pro-contra, ex-cathedra, non-denominational . . . No, hold it. Never mind. The point is that there were a great many strategic things going on down in this vital dirtball region, which is why the Reagan administration called upon its crack intelligence strategists to put down their bananas and get to work. It was clear that we were going to take an active role in the region, a policy that soon led to the turning point in the battle against communist infiltration in the Western Hemisphere, namely:

THE WAR IN GRENADA

This war began when Cuban Communist construction workers began actively engaging in suspected acts of construction on the island of Grenada, which not only contains an abundant natural supply of American medical students but also happens to be in a very strategic and vital location, as we can see from the map on the next page.

Clearly some kind of action had to be taken, and on October 8, it was. Backed by massive sea and air support, nearly two thousand marines stormed onto the island, despite the very real danger that they might sink it. Nevertheless, they were able to overcome not only armed resistance but numerous

GRENADA

(Actual Size)

loose goats, thus winning the war and paving the way for a peace settlement under which we agreed to give the Grenadans upward of $100 million, in return for which they agreed to be our friends, which they still were, we think, last time anybody checked.

Another foreign-policy triumph for Reagan was his 1984 visit to China, where he met for more than three hours with Mao Zedong before realizing that Mao was dead. Aides described the talks as "frank."

This was exactly the kind of firm leadership that Americans had been yearning for, so Reagan was extremely popular when the 1984 presidential election campaign lumbered into view. And once again the Republicans got a lot of help from the

Democrats, who by this point were acting as though they were conducting an experiment to see if it was possible to run a major presidential campaign without winning a single state.

The Democrats nominated Walter Mondale, who immediately announced, in that distinctive voice of his that sounded as if emanating from a nasal passage the size of a gymnasium, that if he were elected, he would jack up taxes. This shrewd move immediately earned him the support of more than half the members of his immediate family, and he went on to lose so badly that people are *still*, years later, showing up at the polls at all hours of the day and night and demanding an opportunity to vote against him.

But Mondale can claim one major achievement: He chose as his running mate Geraldine A. Ferraro, who will become a footnote[4] to history.

THE SECOND REAGAN TERM

The big excitement in the second Reagan term was the "Iran-contra" scandal, which was caused when somebody in the White House, we are still not sure who but *definitely not the president,* decided to sell arms to the Iranian government, which is the same group of greaseballs who took American hostages, which is why we have laws against selling arms to them, but this case was an

[4]Geraldine A. Ferraro.

exception because the money was supposed to go
to either the Sandinistas or maybe the contras,
some strategic group down there, so it was *perfectly OK* to sell the arms, although we wish to
stress once again that *the president knew nothing
about it,* and even if he did he later forgot, which
is no big deal because if a president clutters up his
mind with every pesky little detail such as what
the foreign policy is, he has no room left for important matters.

When news of this got out, there was a big scandal, culminating in marathon hearings by the
Joint House and Senate Committee to Bore Everybody to Death. The highlight of these hearings
was the testimony of Oliver North, a marine lieu-
tenant colonel who was considered the key witness
because he had been singlehandedly operating the
executive branch of the federal government for
several years while everybody else was in meet-
ings. In a dramatic televised moment, North, his
eyes moist and his voice shaking, revealed to the
committee that he was a courageous patriot, after
which he became so overcome by emotion that he
knocked over his bottle of Revlon eye moistener.

Eventually, the nation overcome the trauma of
Iran-contra and went back to reading the sports
pages. And Reagan was soon able to "bounce
back" from the scandal by going to the Soviet
Union, which is in Russia, and signing a historic
agreement with Mikhail Gorbachev that enor-
mously enhanced the prospects for world peace by

prohibiting either side from ever publicly noticing the huge mark on Mr. Gorbachev's head.

Meanwhile, however, new problems were beginning to form. Chief among these was the federal budget deficit, which was mounting at an alarming rate. Both the Reagan administration and the Democratic-controlled Congress had tried a number of possible solutions—increased government spending, having the government spend more money, increasing the amount of money being spent by the government—but that darned ol' deficit just would *not* go away. On top of that, there were other serious problems such as the AIDS epidemic, the Greenhouse Effect, the trade imbalance, drugs, illiteracy, Geraldo Rivera getting his own TV show, and so on. Obviously, the nation was in desperate need of bold new leadership and vision, which was too bad because the next scheduled event was

THE 1988 PRESIDENTIAL ELECTION

This time the Republicans, determined to show the nation that they liked a joke as much as the next person, nominated George Bush, who selected as his running mate young "Dan" Quayle, a Vietnam-era veteran who had received the coveted Round Smiley Face decoration in recognition of the time he accidentally stapled his sleeve to the desk and was trapped for nearly two hours.

Clearly this was a ticket that even the Democrats would have a difficult time losing to, but they worked at it and managed to come up with the ideal candidate in the form of "Mike" Dukakis, a man who, because of a tragic genetic defect, was limited to the same basic range of expressions as an iguana. He'd be making a speech, and he'd start to raise his voice, and it would look like there might be some actual emotion going on inside him, but then suddenly his tongue would flick out to snare a passing insect, and the whole effect would be ruined.

But you also have to give a large pile of credit to Bush and his top political strategist, Darth Vader. Their campaign, conducted via highly informative television commercials, focused on the issues that were certain to be of vital concern to the nation in the years to come, especially:

- The pledge of allegiance.
- Furloughed rapist Willie Horton.
- The budget deficit, and whether it could be corrected by forcing furloughed rapist Willie Horton to say the pledge of allegiance over and over. For fifty years.

When election day rolled around, tens of millions of American voters, impressed by the level of debate, went to the mall. But some of them also cast their ballots, and the Bush-Quayle ticket was swept into office with a clear-cut popular mandate to please not have another election for at least four years.

That is where we stand today. And what lies ahead? Will we be able to solve our social and economic problems, clean up our environment, maybe even improve our technology to the point where we can land a manned spacecraft on Trump? Unfortunately, we cannot know what will happen in the future. If this book proves anything, it's that we don't even know what happened in the *past*.

But we do know this: America is a strong and great country, and her people have withstood many trials and tribulations.[5] And whatever problems lie ahead, we may be sure of one thing: that if we all work together and "hang tough," there will come a day when this nation—maybe not in the next few years; maybe not even in our lifetimes; but someday—will see the end of "Dick" Nixon's political career.

But we wouldn't bet on it.

DISCUSSION QUESTIONS

1. How about we go get a beer?

[5]More tribulations, actually, because many never went to trial.

INDEX

ABOUT THE AUTHOR

DAVE BARRY was described in *The New York Times Book Review* as "the funniest man in America," a claim he has been quick to disavow, except for the plaque on the front door. Nevertheless, the reviewer got there late: The Pulitzer Prize committee had cited him for commentary earlier in 1988, and he got off with an appropriately light sentence.[1] Apart from these facts—which, as Mr. Barry occasionally puts it—we are *not* making up, the relevant details seem to be that he writes for *The Miami Herald* and is syndicated in approximately 150 other newspapers, several of which make money despite this.

Barry lives with his wife, Beth, and son, Robby, in a Coral Gables, Florida, house surrounded by giant mutant spiders.

[1]Even earlier, in 1986, he won the Distinguished Writing Award of the American Association of Newspaper Editors, but what do they know?